D0153532

* *WHERE WILL CONTINUED GROWTH*

What will be the critical constraints ("parameters") affecting
   our future growth?

* *HOW CAN WE ADAPT TO THESE CONSTRAINTS?*

What are our principal "adjustment mechanisms"?
How do they work?
How well do they work under extreme conditions?
What are their shortcomings?
What sorts of costs and risks and time-delays do they involve?
What groups are particular adjustment mechanisms "tilted" toward?
   Or "tilted" against?

DENNIS MEADOWS
Director of the *Limits to Growth* Project

"For most of this century a tacit conspiracy between politicians
and economists has blocked effective discussion of the numerous
questions posed by society's efforts to sustain demographic and
material growth in a finite world. . . . As a consequence mankind
is entering its transition to some sustainable state before even
recognizing the questions whose answers will govern the quality
of life once material growth has ceased. . . . *Growth and Its
Implications for the Future* provides a spectrum of issues that
will rank high on the agenda of anyone concerned about the
viability of the current system."

MAURICE STRONG
Executive Director
United Nations Environment Programme

"I know of no other publication to date which emphasizes more
systematically or extensively, and in such readable form, the
interacting relationships among diverse fields. *Growth and Its
Implications for the Future* also examines and follows mechanisms
for assessing growth problems, weighing both their strengths and
shortcomings."

A REPORT ORIGINALLY PREPARED FOR CONGRESSIONAL HEARINGS

GROWTH
and Its
Implications
for the Future

Elizabeth and David Dodson Gray
William F. Martin

THE DINOSAUR PRESS

Every effort has been made to obtain permission
to reprint cartoons. In several instances artists
could not be located nor could the place of
original publication be identified; permission in
these cases is still sought and artists are asked
to communicate with the authors.

International Standard Book Number 0-915-758-06-7
Library of Congress Catalog Card No. 75-13809

FIRST EDITION

First printing - June 1975
Second printing - May 1976

PRINTED IN THE UNITED STATES OF AMERICA

by The Dinosaur Press (Div. of Readers Press, Inc.)

P.O. Box 666, Branford, Connecticut 06405.

Published simultaneously in Canada and the United States.

To Carroll Wilson
    who inspired our M.I.T. seminar to begin the thinking
And to Frank Potter
    who trusted us to do the writing
We gratefully dedicate this volume
In hope that the future may yet hold promise
    for tomorrow's children
If we act wisely
    today.

Elizabeth Dodson Gray
David Dodson Gray
William F. Martin

Cambridge, Massachusetts

ABOUT THE AUTHORS

David Dodson Gray is a theologian and ethicist
and presently a Research Associate at the Sloan
School of Management, Massachusetts Institute
of Technology. He is the founder of the Boston
Colloquium on "Current Issues in Ethics and
Investments."

Elizabeth Dodson Gray is a theologian and ethicist,
one of whose interests is consciousness-change and
paradigm-change.

William F. Martin is a Program Officer with the
M. I. T. -based Workshop on Alternative Energy
Strategies. Earlier he was a staff member for
the M. I. T. project on Professional Education in
Environmental Management prepared for the
United Nations Environment Programme.

Contents

CONTENTS (Continued)

CONTENTS (Continued)

CONTENTS (Continued)

CONTENTS (Concluded)

PART III.

"I still say there are no limits to growth."

Introduction

"That worries me. There's a ring of authenticity to it!"

The distance we have come since the first Congressional Hearings

on "Growth and Its Implications for the Future" (Spring, 1973)

is suggested by the distance between the cartoon above

("That worries me. There's a ring of authenticity to it! ")

and the cartoon on the previous page

("I still say there are no limits to growth.")

In the cartoon above the "models of doom" have only

the authority of apocalyptic vision;

there is little evidence other than perhaps an inner intuitive resonance.

But in the other cartoon

the heavens themselves are raining tokens that proclaim

it may be later than we think.

> In the pages that follow you will find
> a record and interpretation of
> the continuing consideration being given
> in different quarters to
> "Growth and Its Implications for the Future."
> As you know,
> concern with the implications of future growth
> converges from
> a number of different areas - -
> each of which heretofore has usually been seen
> as more or less separate and independent.
> Here we shall try to see how it all fits together,
> how it all interlocks to speed or brake,
> to stabilize or make unstable
> the process and system
> called Growth.

We shall consider in turn each of these areas as it relates to growth. We will summarize in separate chapters the current state of the growth debate in each field. We will also raise questions of importance to each field as it impinges upon our larger "Growth" concern. We will provide at the end of each chapter a selection of "Readings" that may be used to explore each area in greater detail.

We think it will be helpful, also, to review for you at this point certain basic concepts that have helped us in our own attempts to understand growth. These concepts have been useful to us in simplifying our discussion of the complex phenomena of our world-wide system of growth, and also in focusing our attention upon certain central characteristics of it.

The first concept is EXPONENTIAL GROWTH. Most of the time we are accustomed by our experience to thinking of growth as a linear process, as when you are one year older when another year has elapsed. "A quantity is growing linearly when it increases a constant amount in a constant time period." Exponential growth is quite different. Consider the results of exponential growth in this lily pond that doubles its lilies daily:

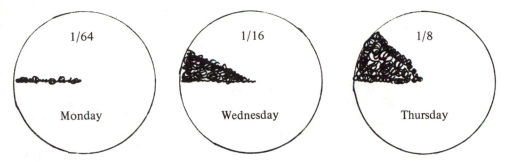

The Lily Pond that Doubles Its Lilies Daily

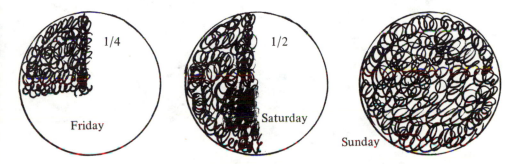

SUNDAY—the day the pond is full of lilies. Monday before—the pond was 63/64ths *empty*.

By Sunday the pond is full of lilies. The Monday before the pond had been 63/64ths empty. "A quantity exhibits exponential growth like this when it increases by a constant percentage of the whole in a constant time period."   Exponential growth is a common process in systems -- biological, financial, and many others -- and is approximated wherever the amount added each year is not constant but continually increases as the total accumulated amount increases.

The importance to us here of exponential growth is this: What is psychologically and physically remote is very close in time. (The pond on Monday was 63/64ths empty, and on Tuesday 62/64ths, so it is difficult to realize that by Sunday, growing at that same exponential growth rate, the pond will have become completely clogged.)   "Saturday" is too late in time for a society to wait to perceive and decide to act upon problems involving exponential growth.

The BIOSPHERE is the term coined
some years ago by the Soviet physicist
Vladimir Ivanovitch Vernadsky for
the biological life-support systems
of the earth that keep alive all that
grows.

The ETHOSPHERE is a cognate term
the Dodson-Grays of our group coined
to describe the life-support systems
of human society -- the values, language,
relationships, institutions, social system,
and so on that comprise human culture,
society, and history.

The biosphere supports physical life.
It is the realm of what we regard as
impersonal. The ethosphere is the
realm of what we regard as personal
rather than impersonal, the realm of
history and society, that sustains,
nourishes and shapes human life.
The terms emphasize the systems
characteristics of our life-settings.
Together the biosphere and ethosphere
comprise the LIFE SYSTEM.

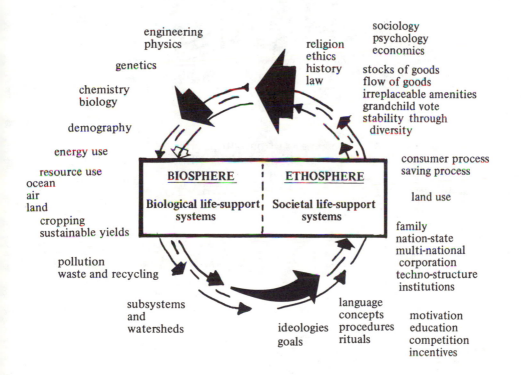

Finally, thinking which is HOLISTIC is concerned with the whole of a complex system (rather than with a part or a subsystem). The term "spaceship Earth" expresses a holistic view of the world as a self-contained life-support vehicle for us all.

"The Kernel . . .

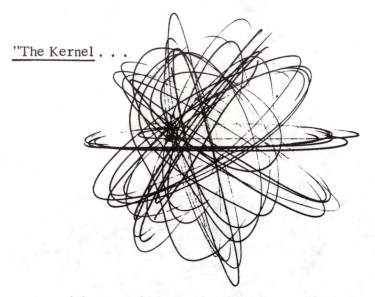

. . . of the incredible tangle of human problems is
      the PRINCIPLE OF INTERRELATEDNESS expressed in . . .
'Everything is connected, ' 'You can never do just one thing, '
'Only one earth. ' "   (Amory Lovins, Nov. 1973)

PART 1

The Parameters of Growth

ECONOMIC GROWTH

ENERGY

POPULATION
FOOD
LAND

RESOURCE
AVAILABILITY

ENVIRONMENTAL
POLLUTION

ENERGY -- A CASE STUDY

1

The Arab oil embargo of October 1973 to
February 1974 catapulted the industrialized
world into awareness of what it would mean
to pull the plug and disconnect the energy
that has fueled our growth.
We were given an experience we could
never have contrived --
an opportunity to glimpse a future
in which energy scarcity combines with
much higher energy prices
to limit growth.
It also limits the social arrangements
that generate and depend on growth.

   Energy questions provide
a good place to begin our thinking
about "Growth and Its Implications for the Future."
The Ford Foundation's Energy Policy Project (EPP)
is a fascinating case study of our
"alternative energy futures."

1.

Three Alternative Energy Futures

The Ford Foundation's Energy Policy Project anticipated the energy limit. The EPP preliminary report (April 1974 -- see "Readings") focuses our attention upon three alternative energy futures* : I. "Business as usual," involving the continuation of historical trends in energy use. (p. 41ff.) II. "Tech Fix Certain," involving systematic application of known (rather than anticipated or merely hoped-for) technology in order to reduce energy use. (p. 45ff.) III. "Zero growth in energy use," involving all the savings of II. plus some life-style changes -- mainly living closer to our work, giving greater reliance to mass transit, making our products more durable, and emphasizing repair, reuse, and recycling. (p. 51ff.)

Question: What do we get for our troubles in each of these scenarios? What is their impact upon growth and upon our future?

* A word about EPP methodology is in order. These futures are not based upon projections of what suppliers such as the AEC or American Petroleum Institute feel they must be ready to produce. Nor are these futures based upon the economy as a whole. Instead EPP examined, industry by industry, how much energy each sector might at most be abl to use (or save). These then are demand futures, built from micro rather than macro projections.

ENERGY USE
in
Q (10^{15}) Btu/ yr.

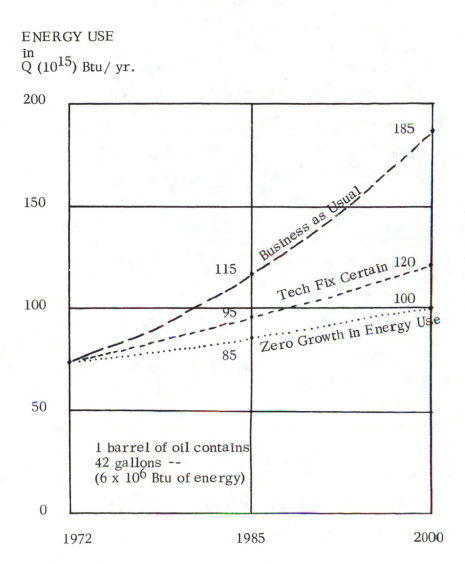

U.S. ALTERNATIVE ENERGY FUTURES

How much will we use?

Data from EPP, Preliminary Report (April 1974)

Chart by David and Elizabeth Dodson Gray

MIT Summary Chart of EPP

	1972	1985	2000	Savings over scenario I at year 2000
I. Business as usual				
3. 8% energy growth rate	72	115	185	--
II. Tech Fix Certain				
apply known technology to increase energy efficiency (no significant life-style changes).	72	95	120	(65)
III. Zero growth in energy use				
certain life-style changes plus Tech Fix of II.	72	85	100	(85)

--more public transit
--live closer to work
--more durable products   all figures in Quadrillions (10^{15})
--three Rs -- repair,   British Thermal Units (Btu)/ year.
    reuse, recycle.   1 Q costs $1 billion at $6/ barrel of oil.

Assumes Census Series E for all scenarios

population	204. 9m	236m	264m
households	69. 2m	79. 9m	98. 7m

2.

Comments on Cost, Environmental Effects, and Employment

Several things are immediately apparent.   One COST COMMENT is that in the year 2000 the cost of energy even at today's prices will be enormous -- and the cost savings of II. and III. are very impressive.   Another cost comment is that the less energy-intensive our national (or regional) economy is, the greater our comparative advantage in cost of goods.

Because of the close linkage between "energy in" and "energy out," there is also an obvious ENVIRONMENTAL COMMENT: the less energy produced, the less the detrimental effects that will result from the production and use of that energy.

Finally there is an interesting EMPLOYMENT COMMENT:
There is a factor of ten separating sectors of the economy requiring

Most Btu per $ value of final product	and	Least Btu
Least jobs per $ value of final product		Most jobs

(See "Options for Energy Conservation, " by Bruce Hannon,
Technology Review, February 1974, p. 25. This is a report
of the study done for EPP. The factor-of-ten figure is based
upon conversations with EPP staff, not the article.)

So, using less energy doesn't necessarily mean less jobs in all
sectors, nor does it necessarily mean less dollar value of final
product in all sectors.

3.
Issues

The three EPP scenarios present alternative futures, each one
of which is limited. These limited-growth futures are limited
in different ways.

Question: In what way is each scenario a limited-growth future?
What limits will do the limiting in the "Business As Usual"
scenario? In the "Tech Fix Certain" scenario? In the
"Zero Growth in Energy Use" scenario?

We will devote the rest of this introduction to the important question
of what may be possible effective limiting factors constraining growth
in any one of these scenarios:

3.1
Will the "effective limit" be a SUPPLY LIMIT upon availability?

Question: Does all that energy exist somewhere? Is that "somewhere"
physically accessible?

Question: Are some of the energy sources so energy-intensive that
little net energy is obtained?

Question: If the energy exists, can we still afford it? If it exists,
will it be profitable to produce or extract it? (Economic limit)

Question: If we need the energy and it exists, will we subsidize
producers to make it attractive (profitable) to supply? If those
who have a supply are in another country or economic or political
block, will they sell it -- or sell it to us -- if it isn't in their
political interest to do so? (Political limit)

Question: Resource Induced Conflict -- RIC -- can take place in order to insure our own supply of a resource or to insure an enemy's non-supply of a resource. What we do not have military power to protect is, in effect, a supply limit. (Military limit)

Question: Will we want to give up what we'll have to in order to get the supply the scenario says we'll use? Will we, for example, sacrifice a prairie society in Wyoming and Montana in order to air-condition Chicago and Washington? (Values limit)

3.2
Will the "effective limit" be a DEMAND LIMIT from users?

Question: Who in the scenario is going to actually use the energy? How much to what sectors? (Sector limits)

Question: Are fewer people going to be working in a given sector in a given scenario? Or are people going to have to get by with less output of that sector per capita? Or even are there going to be fewer people? (Demographic limit)

Question: At higher prices it may not be profitable to use as much energy as one would use at lower price levels. Or it may not be as profitable to produce cheap goods that require large (i.e. expensive) energy inputs. (Economic limit)

Question: Will we use less fossil fuel energy for space heating our homes and offices if we could use solar energy instead? If we insulated better, couldn't we use less energy for space heating or be less cold? (Technology limit)

Question: Won't we have to use less if we must keep reserves for military contingencies? (Military limit)

Question: We will use less energy if we value food from the surface more than the coal gained from strip-mining that surface. If we would rather be warm than mobile, we'll drive less. Or we'll shiver more and continue to be mobile. (Value limit)

Question: Doesn't two or three cars in a suburban garage suggest a life-style that is more energy intensive, perhaps, than a town house near your work? (A demand limit can be rooted in life-styles and patterns of social organization.)

Question: Project Energy Independence is a political goal on the demand side as well as the supply side. (Political limit) Political repression, genocide, and a totalitarian state all can limit demand. (Political limits)

3.3
Checks-and-balances adjustment mechanisms

Supply and demand can be regulated directly by taxation or quotas either upon supply or upon demand or upon both. The market-and-price mechanism tends to regulate supply and demand and tends to decentralize decision-making. (See the section on "Adjustment Mechanisms" about limitations of the market-and-price mechanism.)

Question: What mix of these adjustment mechanisms does each scenario envision?

Question: Are the adjustment mechanisms themselves subject to certain limited usability? (A value bias, for example, against concentrations of power in the marketplace, or against concentrations of power in government.)

Question: Can limits be used to help restrict other limits in a checks-and-balances "systemic" manner?

3.4
Will the "effective limit" within any scenario be an OUTPUT LIMIT upon the environment?

Question: Will thermal pollution be the effective limit for a particular scenario? (Global? Regional? For some cities or rivers or valleys?)

Question: Will by-product pollution be the effective limit? (The coal exists to burn, but can we tolerate the sulpher dioxide in the atmosphere that burning it would put there? Or the nitrous oxide levels from that many cars on a given city's freeways at rush hours?

Question: Will the effective limit be in the trade-off between energy and water? (Colorado shale). Between energy and food? (Wyoming and Montana coal) Between energy and social systems with political clout? (Big city energy needs vs. rural energy sources)

3.5
The systemic limits

Finally the question of "effective limits" comes down to systemic terms.

Question: Is the net addition to supply and to the societal life-support process really worth the environmental costs?

Question: What are the points of diminishing returns? How do we identify them? (Diminishing returns limit)

We would point out the following systemic limits:

-- It is economically unprofitable because it costs more to get it out than we can sell it for. (Economic limit)

-- It is energetically unprofitable because it takes more energy into the process than the energy it produces. (Net energy limit)

-- It is unprofitable in terms of our system-wide life system, because it "costs more" in the quality of life than it "gives back" in quality of life to the system. (Life-system limit)

SELECTED READINGS

Exploring Energy Choices, A Preliminary Report of the Ford Foundation's Energy Policy Project. April 1974.

A Time to Choose: America's Energy Future, Final Report by the Energy Policy Project of the Ford Foundation. Cambridge, Mass.: Ballinger Publishing Co., 1974.

2

RESOURCE AVAILABILITY --
THE "INPUTS" TO OUR LIFE SYSTEM

Our economic and social system depends upon certain crucial material inputs. We are dependent upon steady supplies of such things as fossil fuels, minerals, and metals. When our energy supplies were disrupted in the fall and winter of 1973-74 by the Arab oil embargo, business and jobs were affected. The effect is similar whenever there are spot shortages. The director of the U.S. Geological Survey, V. E. McKelvey, has observed that "even if the economists prove to be right over the long or even the intermediate term, a few years of a 5 percent or 10 percent shortage in any one of many commodities can have serious, even crippling effects." (Letter, Jan. 28, 1974)

RESOURCE AVAILABILITY --

THE "INPUTS" TO OUR LIFE SYSTEM

SUMMARY

1. The Current Context of Shortages

2. Two Different Kinds of Resources

    2.1 Renewable Resources -- our available "income"
    2.2 Nonrenewable Resources -- living off our
         terrestrial "capital"

3. The Current Debate About Future Shortages

    3.1 Will We Run Out of Known or Foreseen Reserves
         of Nonrenewables?
    3.2 Are We in the United States Self-Sufficient?
    3.3 What About Cost?
    3.4 What About the Energy Cost?
    3.5 Net Energy Costs
    3.6 "Entropy" and Availability

1.
The Current Context of Shortages

In an article in Business Week (Nov. 10, 1973) Edwin J. Faster, purchasing agent for Inland Steel, says "There isn't anything not in short supply." The article goes on: "Executives complain about difficulties in obtaining a bewildering array of goods ranging from basic commodities such as oil, steel, cotton, paper, and cement to such manufactured products as plumbing equipment, bearings, motors, and electronic components." (p. 100)

Question: Are such shortages merely short-term? Or do they raise serious questions about the limits to our resources? And in turn, do these current shortages raise questions about our "full speed ahead" policy with growth and our continuing economic development?

Reprinted by permission of Louise Melton

"It's a new game called SHORTAGE, the first person to run out of everything gets to quit playing."

2.
Two Different Kinds of Resources

2.1
Renewable Resources -- Our Available "Income"

When we are talking about supplies of material resources, we need to realize that all material resources are either renewable or nonrenewable. We are able to grow more of our renewable resources. We may be able to discover more of our nonrenewable resources, but we can't grow more. When they are all "used up," they are "gone" (no longer available in a form we can use).

We can "manage" our renewable resources to ensure a continuous or "perpetual" yield, taking each year as a "crop" or harvest only as much as has grown that year. Trees, most food, cattle, wool, cotton, silk -- all these are renewable resources. So are fish and air and soil. Everything that "grows" (has life) depends directly or indirectly upon the chlorophyll cycle that uses solar energy to convert carbon dioxide into sugar and releases oxygen to the atmosphere, converting our current solar-energy "income" into a yearly growth "harvest."

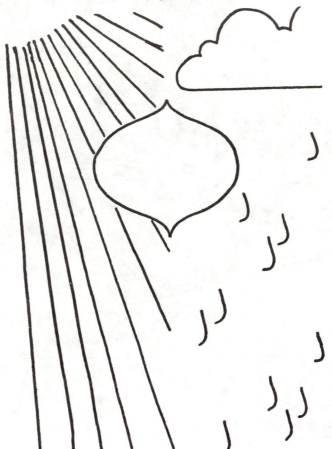

Air, water, and soil are renewable resources even though they don't "live" or "grow." We are dependent upon their being continuously renewed and replenished by cycles powered by the energy of the sun. Here too there is a yearly "harvest" (for example, the annual rainfall) that depends upon a conversion cycle powered by current solar-energy "income." There are also inputs to and resource extractions from the resource base that ought not to exceed the annual renewal capacities. When the capacities of the renewal cycles are exceeded, the result is a degrading or depleting of the renewable-resource base.

Question: Is our growth -- our growing population, our economic
growth, our ever-expanding capital-goods and consumer-goods
needs -- increasing the shortage gap for renewables?
Is our demand for renewables greater than available supplies
of renewables? What does this mean for continued growth?

2.2
Nonrenewable Resources -- Living Off Our Terrestrial "Capital"

Our nonrenewables "are," and we can discover and deplete
them but we can't create or grow them. Our coal and copper and
petroleum and other nonrenewables are our birthright, our inherited
"capital" in the "bank" of spaceship Earth. They are our reserves.
They are a source of subsidy and security that, when used up,
can never be renewed or replaced.

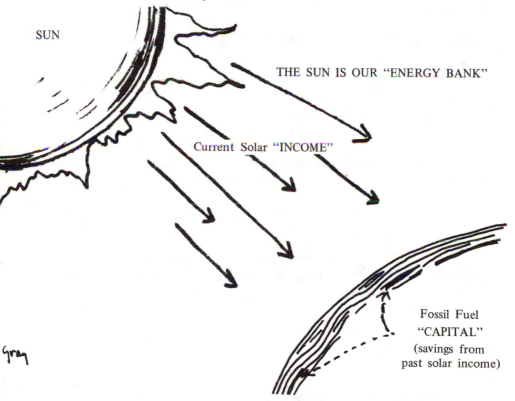

SUN

THE SUN IS OUR "ENERGY BANK"

Current Solar "INCOME"

Fossil Fuel
"CAPITAL"
(savings from
past solar income)

Our nonrenewable resources are of two sorts. Our fossil
fuels (petroleum, coal, natural gas) are reserves or savings
from previous solar-energy income. Green plants that grew
long ago became the fossil fuels we can find and can use today.
Our other sort of nonrenewable resource is the minerals and metals
and gases (helium, argon, et al.) which are our earth's crust.
They are concentrated in known and unknown places and quantities
in that crust.

3.
The Current Debate about Future Shortages

3.1
Will we run out of known or foreseen reserves of nonrenewables?

For nonrenewables the crucial questions are:

Question: How large are our reserves?

Question: How long will our reserves last?

Question: How "available" are they?

Question: What are the critical "run-out points" for our U.S. economy?

Some data suggest that at current usage rates many nonrenewables will be depleted early in the next century. (Current usage rates represent, in the vocabulary of the Ford Foundation Energy Policy Project, "zero growth in usage rates" -- i.e. the farther out or longer life-expectancy of our reserves.)

Other data suggest that at the current rate at which our use of materials is going up many of these nonrenewable resources will not last out this century. (This is the "business as usual" or historic growth rates scenario of EPP. -- i.e. the shorter life-expectancy of our reserves.)

For convenience in notation, future reserves at zero-growth in usage rates are called "static reserves." Future reserves at historic (i.e. exponential) growth rates are called "exponential reserves." These approximate probable upper and lower limits to our reserves.

How is such a calculation made? The world's stocks of most minerals is known with a fair degree of accuracy. Thus we can begin the calculation knowing how much of a resource we have. We know, too, the rate at which it is being consumed. By relating the rate of consumption to the quantity in reserve we can calculate the number of years the reserve will last. This figure is known as the static reserve index (SRI). The SRI is the figure often quoted for the lifetime of resources. However, the rate of consumption is not a constant. If it is related to industrial and population growth, together with the trend it has shown over a number of years, and this new value is compared with the known reserve, the resulting lifetime for the resource is known as the Exponential Reserve Index (ERI). An exponential growth in demand will reduce the lifetime of a reserve by a very large factor. If, for example, we take a resource with an SRI of 10,000 years and then assume an exponential increase in the rate of consumption of 2 per cent per year, the ERI is 250 years! If, at some stage before the stocks are exhausted completely, the reserve that remains is doubled – let us assume that new sources are discovered, or there is a major breakthrough in extraction technology which permits us to mine reserves that were previously uneconomic – the effect is to add seventy-five years to the ERI. In other words, doubling the stocks may add no more than seventy-five years to the time taken to use up the resource completely. The cost of extracting the resource can also be estimated and it is found, not surprisingly, that as the reserves are reduced – the most easily accessible being used first – the cost rises exponentially.

SRIs and ERIs have been compared for a number of resources. The results are disturbing:

	SRI years	ERI years
Aluminium	175	34
Chromium	560	92
Coal	900	595
Cobalt	155	45
Copper	40	25
Gold	17	14
Iron	400	73
Lead	15	12
Manganese	160	49
Mercury	13	13
Molybdenum	100	27
Natural gas	35	14
Nickel	140	30
Petroleum	70	20
Platinum	20	12
Silver	20	17
Tin	25	17
Tungsten	40	36
Zinc	18	16

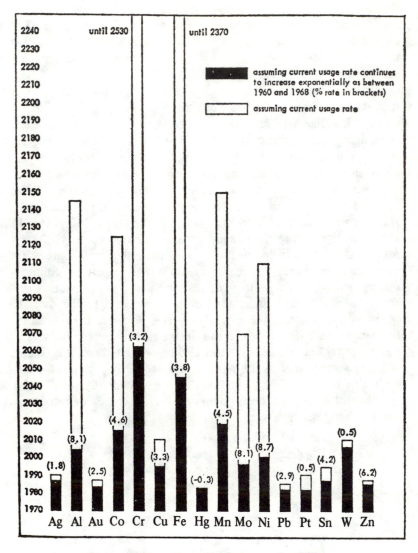

Static and exponential reserves of metals.

Chart: "A Blueprint for Survival," p. 7
Table and Text: *Who Will Eat?*
by Michael Allaby, pp. 39-40.

V.E. McKelvey, the director of the U.S. Geological Survey, summarized the state of U.S. reserves and resources of each mineral in commercial use:

> For some of the metals in which United States production has been small or nonexistent for many years -- tin, chrome, mercury, and the platinum metals -- we have small or negligible reserves, and little potential.
>
> For other metals -- copper, zinc, lead, manganese, nickel tungsten, gold, and silver -- presently mineable reserves plus estimated resources are roughly equivalent to what the Bureau of Mines has estimated to be the cumulative demand between now and the end of the century.
>
> Only for a few metals -- iron, aluminum, magnesium, molybdenum, rhenium, titanium, vanadium, uranium, and thorium -- are there reserves and resources, including presently subeconomic as well as undiscovered resources, that appear sufficient to meet projected future demands for more than a hundred years.
>
> For fossil fuels, the picture is similar. We still have a potential for oil and gas in the form of now uneconomic and undiscovered resources, but the potential is huge only for coal and oil shale.
>
> With a few exceptions, such as fluorite and asbestos, domestic reserves of the nonmetallic minerals are adequate for the next several decades and the potential for future development is large.
>
> . . . For some minerals that are in short supply in the United States, world resources are comparatively much larger. But qualitatively the entire picture is somewhat similar to that just described for the United States. Identified and undiscovered reserves and resources for most minerals are adequate for anticipated world demand only for the next several decades and resources of only a few minerals appear sufficient to last for a century or longer.

(Speech: "Potential Mineral Reserves," Jan. 17, 1974. Italics added. See "Readings.")

3.2
Are we in the U.S. self-sufficient?

Our U.S. birthright is rich in minerals but in the 1920s the U.S. began to be a net importer of minerals, and now we derive more than half of our mineral supplies from abroad. Nicholas Wade (in Science, Jan. 18, 1974) points out that our dependency upon mineral imports makes the U.S. "more vulnerable to Third World cartels." Congresswoman Patsy T. Mink, chairperson of the Subcommittee on Mines and Mining of the House Interior and Insular Affairs Committee recently said the increasing competion for world mineral supplies could permit exporting nations "to cut off the sale of minerals to the United States while at the same time not sacrificing their economic well-being." (Mar. 29, 1974, Congressional Quarterly, Apr. 6, 1974, p. 895.)

Table 1. Percentage of U.S. mineral requirements imported during 1972. (Data derived from Mining and Minerals Policy 1973, a report by the Secretary of the Interior to the Congress).

Mineral	Percentage imported	Major foreign sources
Platinum group metals	100	U.K., U.S.S.R., South Africa, Canada, Japan, Norway
Mica (sheet)	100	India, Brazil, Malagasy
Chromium	100	U.S.S.R., South Africa, Turkey
Strontium	100	Mexico, Spain
Cobalt	98	Zaire, Belgium, Luxembourg, Finland, Canada, Norway
Tantalum	97	Nigeria, Canada, Zaire
Aluminum (ores and metal)	96	Jamaica, Surinam, Canada, Australia
Manganese	95	Brazil, Gabon, South Africa, Zaire
Fluorine	87	Mexico, Spain, Italy, South Africa
Titanium (rutile)	86	Australia
Asbestos	85	Canada, South Africa
Tin	77	Malaysia, Thailand, Bolivia
Bismuth	75	Mexico, Japan, Peru, U.K., Korea
Nickel	74	Canada, Norway
Columbium	67	Brazil, Nigeria, Malagasy, Thailand
Antimony	65	South Africa, Mexico, U.K., Bolivia
Gold	61	Canada, Switzerland, U.S.S.R.
Potassium	60	Canada
Mercury	58	Canada, Mexico
Zinc	52	Canada, Mexico, Peru
Silver	44	Canada, Peru, Mexico, Honduras, Australia
Barium	43	Peru, Ireland, Mexico, Greece
Gypsum	39	Canada, Mexico, Jamaica
Selenium	37	Canada, Japan, Mexico, U.K., Peru, Canada
Tellurium	36	Peru, Canada
Vanadium	32	South Africa, Chile, U.S.S.R.
Petroleum (includes liquid natural gas)	29	Central and South America, Canada, Middle East
Iron	28	Canada, Venezuela, Japan, Common Market (EEC)
Lead	26	Canada, Australia, Peru, Mexico
Cadmium	25	Mexico, Australia, Belgium, Luxembourg, Canada, Peru
Copper	18	Canada, Peru, Chile
Titanium (ilmenite)	18	Canada, Australia
Rare earths	14	Australia, Malaysia, India
Pumice	12	Greece, Italy
Salt	7	Canada, Mexico, Bahamas
Cement	5	Canada, Bahamas, Norway
Magnesium (nonmetallic)	8	Greece, Ireland
Natural gas	9	Canada
Rhenium	4	West Germany, France
Stone	2	Canada, Mexico, Italy, Portugal

3.3
What about cost?

Question: Have we moved from a buyer's market to a seller's
market?   Can we expect other export cartels than OPEC
also to double or triple prices or cut production by half
or two-thirds or both -- so that their annual dollar income
remains constant while the duration of that income level is
doubled or tripled.   (See the debate among Steven Krasner,
Zuhayr Mikdashi, and C. Fred Bergsten, Foreign Policy,
March 1974, in "Readings.")

Question: Can we afford the dollars to buy at these prices? Will it
be profitable to find and develop our own alternate sources?
Or sources for substitutes?

3.4
What about the Energy Cost?

Question: We must ask finally not just about the cost in dollars
but the energy cost.   Are we going to want to afford the energy
inputs to get energy or other resources which exist but are not
readily available? For example, the shale oil is there, the
Wyoming and Montana coal is there; but it will cost at least
three times what oil has in the past cost (in dollars) to get out.
The net energy cost is much greater.

3.5
Net Energy Costs

Howard T. Odum has pointed out that "We are still expanding our
rate of consumption of gross energy, but since we are feeding a
higher and higher percentage back into the energy-seeking process,
we are decreasing our percentage of net energy production."
(See "Energy, Ecology and Economics" in the "Readings.")

Net energy is like net profit: increasing gross sales (or gross energy
output) makes sense only if it increases net profit (net energy).
Net energy is the energy you produce, minus the energy you used
producing it.   (See "It Takes Energy To Produce Energy: The Net's
The Thing," by Edward Flattau and Jeff Stansbury, in the "Readings.")

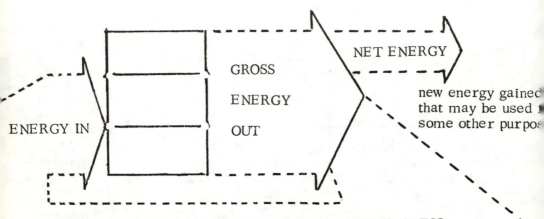

ENERGY REQUIRED TO DEVELOP AND RUN THE PROCESS

    (to develop the technology to do it
    (to train researchers to develop the technology
    (to sustain the researchers from birth through training to development
      and the energy after development
    (to produce the machinery, deliver it to site, and
    (get it to markets where it will be used.

Question: What is the relation of "dollar inflation of prices" to the
net energy concept, and to its corollary of diminishing returns
in net energy?

Question: Is the market-and-price mechanism rigged so as to mask
energy-based accounting costs? Is what we see as dollar inflation
that mask? (See "Cosmic Energetics," prepared by The Center
for Applied Energetics, Office of the Governor, State of Oregon,
March 1974. See "Readings" on "Market-and-Price Mechanism.")

3.6
"Entropy" and Availability

"Gone . . ."*

Strictly speaking, we do not "destroy" the portions of our environment which we use for our comfort and convenience; instead these commodities simply become unavailable for our further use.

Energy for example can be neither created nor destroyed but energy can be transmitted to another place or changed to another form. Thus when we burn coal, the chemical energy released as heat ultimately will be lost to outer space or result in a rise in the temperature of our surroundings.

Likewise a mineral resource upon being used may be mixed with other materials to the extent that it is no longer economic to recover it. For example, nearly every iron atom which was present in the earth in prehistoric times is still in or on the earth.

This basic continuity of energy when extended to mass-energy constitutes a cornerstone of physics known as the Law of Conservation of Energy, or as the First Law of Thermodynamics.

"Entropy" -- a measure of the unavailability or "goneness"

Several important attributes of nature are describable in terms of a property known as entropy, a quality of our environment which measures (a) the extent to which energy and/or resources are available to us, or (b) the extent to which one finds materials and energy either aggregated on the one hand or in disorder on the other. Thus coal, a package of available energy, is an aggregate of carbon atoms which, when burned, becomes a cloud of carbon dioxide and heat.

By virtue of the way scientists define entropy, entropy increases as materials and energy become unavailable or as aggregation is replaced by disorder. Experience shows, furthermore, that all processes in Nature are accompanied by an increase in the total entropy of the universe; resources and energy always become unavailable, order is always replaced by disorder.

Science knows of no process in Nature in which net regeneration of order or availability is taking place. We can produce local increases in order (we can manufacture a very ordered cluster of iron, copper, and carbon atoms called a Cadillac) but the net change in the process is an unrecoverable loss of availability of materials and a very large loss in the availability of energy. This observation of the direction of all events in Nature is known as the Entropy Law, or the Second Law of Thermodynamics.

* The sections on *entropy* (including the Humpty Dumpty analogy) are by Joseph W. Straley, Professor of Physics, University of North Carolina at Chapel Hill -- and a member of the M.I.T. group during his sabbatical.

Humpty Dumpty and "Entropy"

Before Humpty Dumpty fell off the wall,
Humpty Dumpty's components were ordered (arranged)
the way Humpty Dumpty liked.

When Humpty Dumpty had his great fall,
Humpty Dumpty was "conserved" -- nothing was lost
    (First Law of Thermodynamics)
But "disordered."
    (Second Law of Thermodynamics)

*Concept and Visual by
Joseph W. Straley*

Humpty Dumpty's components did not any longer have
the useful physical ordering Humpty Dumpty liked.

and

This change from Order to Disorder brings Us Easily to

ENTROPY -- A Measure of the LOSS of ORDER

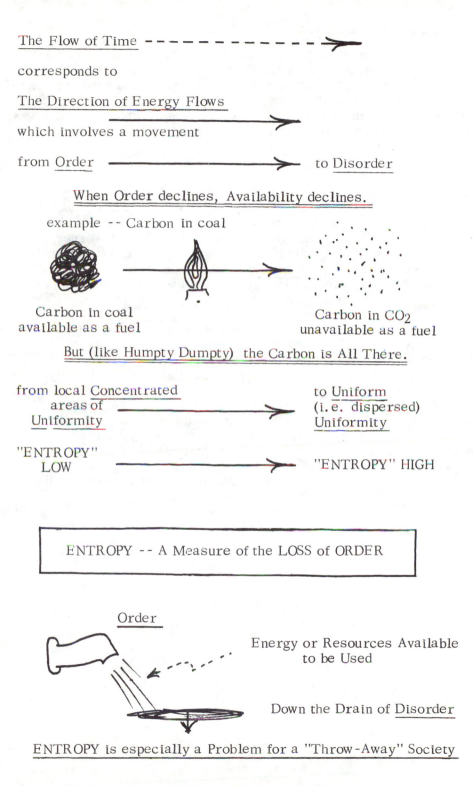

The Flow of Time -- -- -- -- -- -->

corresponds to

The Direction of Energy Flows

which involves a movement

from Order ---------> to Disorder

When Order declines, Availability declines.

example -- Carbon in coal

Carbon in coal
available as a fuel

Carbon in CO_2
unavailable as a fuel

But (like Humpty Dumpty) the Carbon is All There.

from local Concentrated
areas of ---------->
Uniformity

to Uniform
(i.e. dispersed)
Uniformity

"ENTROPY"
LOW ---------->

"ENTROPY" HIGH

ENTROPY -- A Measure of the LOSS of ORDER

Order

Energy or Resources Available
to be Used

Down the Drain of Disorder

ENTROPY is especially a Problem for a "Throw-Away" Society

Not "Is It There?" but "To What Extent Is It Available?"

Energy as found in Nature must be converted into a form in which it is useful to Man. (For example, a barrel of crude oil left to its own devices cannot motivate a plow.) Several conversion processes therefore take place as one traces a fuel from the mine or well to the point of application. Each of these processes involves a very significant increase in total entropy, that is, in a decrease in the availability of resources and energy.

At the present stage of science and engineering, for example, less than a fourth of the chemical energy of oil or coal is ever recovered as useful work. This is the situation because industrial operations involve one conversion process that is grossly and inherently inefficient, namely, the conversion of thermal energy (the output of coal or uranium) into mechanical energy (the output of the turbine). Even the theoretical maximum efficiency of this entropy-enhancing process is only 40% for fossil-fueled engines or 33% for uranium-fueled engines.

The entropy-enhancing nature of the required conversion process is frequently ignored when enthusiastic partisans for some given form of energy cite simply the energy contained by the material while ignoring essential facts about its availability.

For example, there well may be more thermal energy in the ocean and more chemical energy in our oil shale than is found stored in all Middle East oil. The question to ask, however, is not simply "Is it there?" but also "To what extent is it available?" We will not come to grips with our environment until we have fully grasped the lessons which are implicit in the limitations described by the Law of Entropy.

SELECTED READINGS

Overview

Brown, Lester R., "The World Resources Shortage To Change Lifestyles, International Relations." International <u>Herald Tribune</u>, Nov. 26, 1973.

Long-Term Availability -- Two Views

Malenbaum, Wilfred, "Resource Shortages in an Expanding World." <u>Wharton Quarterly,</u> Winter 1973.

McKelvey, V. E., "Potential Mineral Reserves." A speech presented at AIME Mining Symposium, Duluth, Minn., Jan. 17, 1974.

<u>Mineral Resources and the Environment.</u> Washington, D.C.: National Academy of Sciences, 1975.

Third World Cartels

<u>Foreign Policy</u> special section, "One, Two, Many OPEC's . . . ?" Spring 1974.

Mikdashi, Zuhayr, "Collusion Could Work."
Krasner, Stephen D., "Oil Is The Exception."
Bergsten, C. Fred, "The Threat Is Real."

Wade, Nicholas, "Raw Materials: U.S. Grows More Vulnerable to Third World Cartels." <u>Science</u>, Jan. 18, 1974.

Managing in a Shortage Economy

<u>Business Week</u> special section, "Managing In A Shortage Economy." Nov. 10, 1973.

Net Energy Concept

Flattau, Edward and Jeff Stansbury, "It Takes Energy To Produce Energy: The Net's The Thing." <u>Congressional Record</u>, Mar. 8, 1974.

Odum, Howard T., "Energy, Ecology, and Economics." <u>Ambio</u>, 1973.

3

ENVIRONMENTAL POLLUTION---

THE "OUTPUTS" FROM OUR LIFE SYSTEM

WHAT IS THE USE OF A HOUSE IF YOU HAVEN'T GOT A TOLERABLE PLANET TO PUT IT ON?

-THOREAU

Jim Steinmeyer

ENVIRONMENTAL POLLUTION --

THE "OUTPUTS" FROM OUR LIFE SYSTEM

SUMMARY

1. The Debate

2. Seeing the Global Picture -- SCEP (1970) and SMIC (1971)

3. Sources of Pollution

    3.1 "Recyclables" vs. "Nonrenewables"
        among the outputs of our life system

4. Environmental "Sinks"

    4.1 The Atmosphere as a Sink
    4.2 Bodies of Water as a Sink

5. Some Crucial Problems

    5.1 Toxic Substances
    5.2 Man-made Toxic Substances
    5.3 The Search for Energy Sources

6. How Can We Adjust Our System To Protect Our Environment?

    6.1 Monitoring
    6.2 Adjustment Proposals
        6.2.1 Input Adjustment Mechanisms -- Wellhead and Mine
        6.2.2 Controlling Wastes at the Useful-Product Output
        6.2.3 Consumer Adjustments
        6.2.4 Governmental Adjustments

7. Adjustments in Our Thinking

    7.1 From "Isolated Problems" to "Holistic Thinking"
    7.2 From "Limits" to "Givens"

1.
The Debate

Environmental pollution is often the first agenda item when the pros and cons of growth are discussed. At issue is what the "outputs" from our life system and its growth are doing to the life-setting of that system.

Environmentalists argue that increased growth will lead to increased environmental degradation. The other view is stated by an industry research group, the Committee for Economic Development (CED), that contends "It is a mistake to believe that stopping or reversing economic growth will automatically improve the environment. On the contrary, a healthy rate of growth is prerequisite for carrying the costs of a rigorous program of environmental protection." ("More Effective Programs for a Cleaner Environment," April 1974. See "Readings.")

The following questions point to a possible middle position in this debate:

Question: In what ways can America continue economic growth without seriously harming the environment?

Question: In what ways can we continue to have environmental "health" without seriously damaging our social and economic system?

Question: Are we using the most socially and economically effective ways to control pollution and to achieve a healthy natural environment in the United States?

Question: Are there ways in which our social and economic institutions should change in order to be developing machinery for protecting our environment?

Question: How best do we proceed to balance the fragilities of our social and economic institutions with the fragilities we face in our natural environment?

2.
Seeing the Global Picture -- SCEP (1970) and SMIC (1971)

"The Study of Critical Environmental Problems" (SCEP) was a one-month conference of more than seventy scientists whose purpose was to focus upon "environmental problems whose cumulative effects on ecological systems are so large and prevalent that they have worldwide significance." "The existence of a global problem," the SCEP report is careful to point out, "does not imply the

Langley in the Christian Science Monitor. © 1973 TCSPS

necessity for a global solution. The sources of pollution are activities of man that can often be effectively controlled or regulated where they occur."

SCEP looked at both climatic effects and ecological effects. The major conclusions were that despite the basic stability of climatic and ecological systems in the past, human activity is now modifying these systems. The study notes "the deficiencies in the data and projections related to problems of global concern." As a result there is currently an inadequate foundation for definitive statements about environmental effects.

Nonetheless SCEP found it possible already to identify some of the important "leverage points" at which human activity is modifying our global climate and ecology. SCEP identifies next steps, highlighting especially those that cut across traditional areas of environmental responsibility.

The 1971 "Study of Man's Impact on Climate" (SMIC) was a three-week review by thirty scientists from fourteen countries aimed at "providing an international scientific consensus on what we know and do not know and how to fill the gaps" on inadvertent climate modification issues that would necessarily have to involve multinational cooperation.

SMIC has prepared the definitive assessment of the present state of scientific understanding of the possible impacts of man's activities on the regional and global climate. The following major areas have been covered by their assessment:

-- Previous climate changes
-- Man's activities influencing climate
-- Theory and models of climate change
-- Climatic effects of man-made surface change
-- Modification of the troposphere (surface air)
-- Modification of the stratosphere

(See the "Readings" for a summary of SCEP and SMIC findings and recommendations.)

3.
Sources of Pollution

We have to think of environmental pollution not only in terms of where it ends up ("sinks") but also in terms of where it comes from ("sources"). All our inputs to our life system eventually become the outputs of our life system. Wastes and residues are generated at all points in a product's (or a person's) life -- in the extraction of raw materials, in the transporting of them, in the industrial process (and industrial disposal), in the commercial process of its sale, in the consumer's use of the product, and finally in the consumer's disposal of it after its useful life. "Damage to physical and biological systems from waste must be recognized and minimized at every step from mine to ultimate consumer." (National Commission on Materials Policy)

ENVIRONMENTAL ("output") POLLUTION

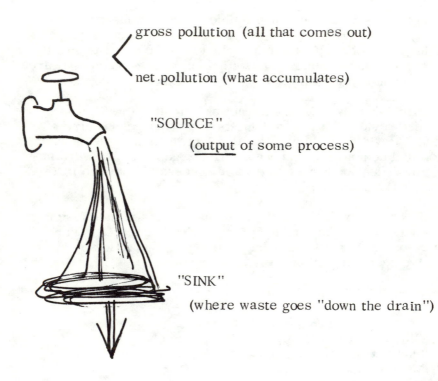

gross pollution (all that comes out)

net pollution (what accumulates)

"SOURCE"

(output of some process)

"SINK"

(where waste goes "down the drain")

3.1
"Recyclables" vs. "Nonrenewables" among the outputs of our life system*

Prior to the time that Man came to dominate the biosphere (roughly one hundred years ago with the advent of the Industrial Revolution), nearly everything was recycled. Plants and animals, including Man, used the portion of biosphere they needed, and returned the residuals which we now call waste to the biosphere.

* We are indebted to Prof. Joseph W. Straley for the wording of this section.

Through the action of other organisms and the sun, these materials continued a useful relationship with other materials in a nearly steady-state manner.

The notion of waste became important when man began to use selected materials at such prodigious rates and in such large quantities as to overwhelm all the natural processes by which recycling has always taken place. (It is ironic that so many of us today tend to think of recycling as an activity Man recently invented.) It now is clear that recycling has always occurred, but that the environment can no longer respond to man's "insults" as rapidly as he now delivers them.

Many of the residues generated through our use of components of our environment we manage to get back to a constructive relation- ship with the biosphere. These residues we call "recyclables." Where we have failed to do the simple things that would put a given residue into such a constructive relationship with the biosphere, that material becomes a pollutant.

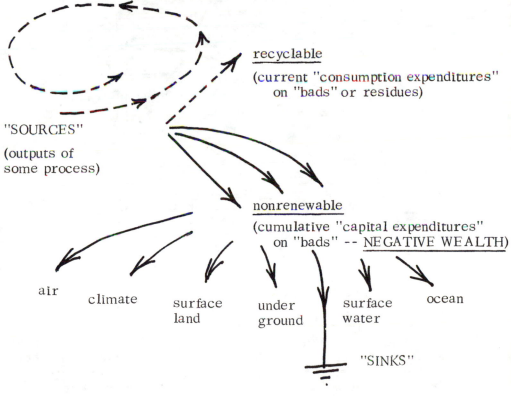

recyclable

(current "consumption expenditures" on "bads" or residues)

"SOURCES"

(outputs of some process)

nonrenewable

(cumulative "capital expenditures" on "bads" -- NEGATIVE WEALTH)

air   climate   surface land   under ground   surface water   ocean

"SINKS"

The Flow of Substances Into Some Part of the Environment

Most of the materials we extract from the biosphere are diverted from their normal role in nature to roles that serve the convenience of Man. In the process these materials are degraded, either by undergoing chemical reactions with other materials (coal becomes carbon dioxide) or are diffused beyond hope of recovery (the metal worn from a bearing will never be available for recycling). These materials are the "nonrenewables," because we remove them from further access for all time.

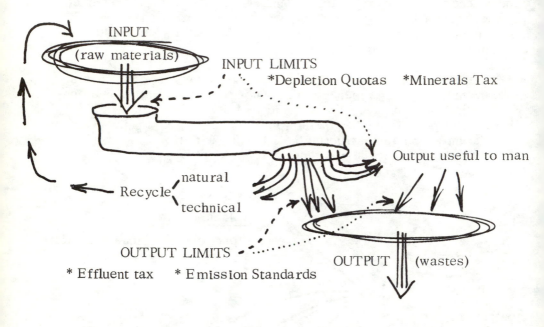

INPUT
(raw materials)

INPUT LIMITS
*Depletion Quotas   *Minerals Tax

Output useful to man

natural
Recycle
technical

OUTPUT LIMITS
* Effluent tax   * Emission Standards

OUTPUT   (wastes)

Flow Diagram of Materials from Input to Waste Output
showing
The Points at which the Impact of the Process upon Environment
Can Be Constrained.

4.
Environmental "Sinks"

There really isn't, in Garrett Hardin's words, "any 'away' to throw things to," so there are a limited number of "sinks" for our wastes or residues to go to. They can be vented to the atmosphere; they can be washed away in water (into ocean, surface waters, or underground waters); they can be deposited on, in or under the ground's topsoil.

The SCEP report observes: "The health and vigor of ecological systems are easily reduced if (1) general and widespread damage occurs to the predators, (2) substantial numbers of species are lost, or (3) general biological activity is depressed. Most pollutants that affect life have some effect on all three processes." Hence SCEP recommends both "an intensive program of technology assessment" of wastes (sources, kinds, rates, toxic effects, low levels of chronic exposure) and "a systematic program of environmental assessment" of the "routes of distribution of pollutants, their eventual distribution in the environment, and their passage through ecosystems." (p. 23)

4.1
The Atmosphere as a Sink

We release heat, gases, and particles to the atmosphere. Locally these are the heat islands around our cities, the smog that makes our eyes run, the photochemical pollutants that change our rain into a dilute acid, and the soot and dirt that foul our buildings and our clothes. At the regional and global level the problem to

"Just for the record, who was the wise guy that thought up 'No Deposit, No Return'?"

Reprinted by permission of Sidney Harris

which SCEP and especially SMIC addressed themselves was the effects of these pollutants on the complex feedback systems which maintain the global energy and temperature balance between incoming solar energy and the energy the earth radiates back into space.

Man introduces significant quantities of sulfates, nitrates and hydrocarbons into the atmosphere. The optical properties of these particles and how they scatter and absorb energy from the sun and the surface of the earth must be studied, improved techniques must be developed, and specific particle content must be monitored to improve our understanding of their impact.

(An EPA summary of SCEP conclusions in Alternative Futures and Environmental Quality, Environmental Protection Agency, Office of Research and Development. May 1973. p. 89.)

The SCEP and SMIC reports describe the delicate thermal balance that accompanies the complex climatic features of the earth and outline the role of ocean currents and air currents, of evaporation and precipitation, and of reflection and absorption of solar energy in maintaining that balance.

The currently most sensitive point in the atmosphere-and-climate system seems to be the Arctic icecap, whose melting (or extension) would quickly affect (and in other ages has affected) global thermal balance and thus climates. The gradual changes in the composition of our atmosphere is another point of great potential risk over the longer term because "should man ever be compelled to stop producing carbon dioxide no coal, oil, or gas could be burned and all industrial societies would be drastically affected." (SCEP, p. 11f. -- "Readings")

4.2
Bodies of Water as a Sink

We are all familiar with the problems which arise from the use of our lakes and streams and coastal waters as a sink for our wastes. The lake fills with grasses because it gets too much fertilizer runoff from nearby farms, or the river fish die for lack of oxygen because of phosphates from laundry detergents. The materials we dump in our rivers result in lead in our shell fish and mercury in our swordfish.

Our use of water as a sink generates two quite different sorts of problems. On the one hand life systems within the water can be overfertilized so that the natural system-balance is destroyed: "Eutrophication of waters through overfertilization (principally with phosphorus and nitrogen) produces an excess of organic matter that decomposes, removing oxygen and killing the fish." (SCEP, p. 26)

On the other hand, marine organisms, feeding upon one another, reconcentrate substances which are very dispersed in the water. The life processes function naturally -- and carry with them substances which with chronic exposure are toxic at quite low concentrations.

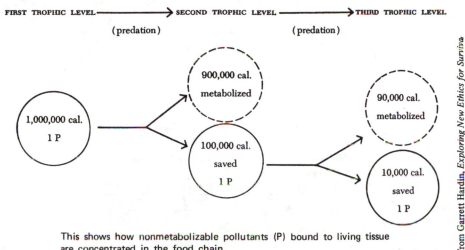

FIRST TROPHIC LEVEL ⟶ SECOND TROPHIC LEVEL ⟶ THIRD TROPHIC LEVEL

(predation)   (predation)

1,000,000 cal. 1 P

900,000 cal. metabolized

100,000 cal. saved 1 P

90,000 cal. metabolized

10,000 cal. saved 1 P

from Garrett Hardin, *Exploring New Ethics for Survival*

This shows how nonmetabolizable pollutants (P) bound to living tissue are concentrated in the food chain.

Water is not only a sink; it is also a part of a number of more complex global systems. When pollutants, for example oil spilled in the water or soot settling out of the air, facilitate the melting of the Arctic icecap, this will have an effect upon the atmosphere, upon the climate, upon radiation and reflection of solar energy in the Arctic region and hence upon global heat transfers and finally upon global weather patterns. (See SCEP and SMIC.)

5.
Some Crucial Problems

5.1
Toxic Substances

The swordfish market was devastated by the discovery that mercury often concentrated in the swordfish in ways that were not fatal to swordfish but were a hazard to humans. The mercury released from manufacturing processes into waterways each year is sizable in tonnage but still very small compared to the volume of water in the oceans of the world.

But mercury, lead and other heavy and toxic metals that are present in the oceans only in trace amounts are reconcentrated by a combination of the biological life processes and the feeding levels by which larger animals take into their bodies all the trace metals in the flesh of the smaller animals they eat.

The longer the food chain, the greater the concentration of toxic substances.

5.2
Man-made Hazardous Substances

Each year chemists produce more than a thousand new substances (Amory Lovins). No one knows the long-term side effects of any of these. The biologist Garrett Hardin has pointed out that, while we protect human beings by the assumption that they are innocent until proven guilty, we must maintain this policy of protecting those same human beings against organic compounds' unforeseen toxic side effects by holding the chemical compound "guilty until proven innocent." The need for such a policy is underscored by the recent information about the hazards of asbestos fibers and polyvinyl chloride fumes.

Lovins points out that "Identifying and regulating toxic, mutagenic, tetrogenic, carcinogenic, and other hazardous substances grows steadily more urgent." (See "Long-Term Constraints on Human Activity" in the "Readings." See also the two subsequent reports by the National Academy of Sciences on Principles for Evaluating Chemicals in the Environment and Assessing Potential Ocean Pollutants.)

5.3
The Search for Energy Sources

A particularly relevant issue in the immediate future is the amount of environmental degradation we will generate in our search for ways to increase our energy supply. Robert Cahn, the environmental editor of the Christian Science Monitor, summed it up: "Almost everything that increases energy supply or uses energy pollutes air or water, adds to solid waste, disrupts land or threatens wildlife." (Dec. 20, 1973)

IT BECAME NECESSARY TO DESTROY THE ENVIRONMENT TO SAVE IT...

Editorial cartoon by Paul Conrad. Copyright, Los Angeles Times. Reprinted with permission.

6.
How Can We Adjust Our System
To Protect Our Environment?

6.1
Monitoring

To know what to do for our environment, it is necessary to know what is happening in it and to understand the significance of what is happening. "A major conclusion of the SCEP study was that data of all types was lacking and that new methods of collecting, compiling and standardizing data are required." (EPA Alternative Futures and Environmental Quality, May 1973.) We might well ask ourselves the following questions

Question: What are the critical points in the environmental system which must be monitored?

Question: How would you set up an effective monitoring system? What kind of data would you need? What sort of people? How are they trained?

Question: How much of a budget would an effective monitoring system need?

Question: How would the results of the monitoring be translated into effective adjustment action?

The primary recommendations of the SCEP conference were about monitoring:

1. . . . development of new methods for gathering and compiling global economic and statistical information, which organize data across traditional areas of environmental responsibility.

2. . . . international physical, chemical, and ecological measurement standards . . . a monitoring standards center with a "real time" data analysis capacity, allowing for prompt feedback to monitoring units.

3. . . . integration of existing and planned monitoring programs.

(Full text in SCEP report, p. 7 in "Readings.")

6.2
Adjustment Proposals

The National Commission on Materials has pointed out that "damage to physical and biological systems from waste must be recognized and minimized at every step from mine to ultimate consumer."

<u>Question:</u> What is the right mix of adjustment mechanisms?

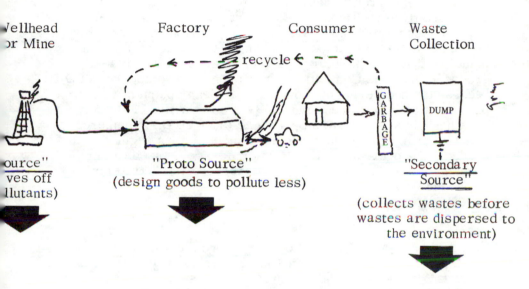

The Types of Sources of Pollution

6.2.1

Input Adjustment Mechanisms -- Well Head and Mine

Depletion quotas are not new to this country. For many years the amount of oil a producer could produce in a month was regulated by state commissions in order to keep the price of oil high. Today depletion quotas provide a possible "valve" for keeping the inputs to the economic system at a point which will minimize environmental degradation. The economist Herman E. Daly has advocated such controls. (A section on "Constant Physical Wealth" in an article "The Steady-State Economy" reprinted in "Readings.")

6.2.2
Controlling Wastes at the Useful-Product Output

Another point at which regulation can
occur is the point at which there is a useful-
product output -- the industrial process level.
Regulation here can affect either the industrial
process and its wastes, or the design of the
product (e.g., an auto) and the waste its
subsequent use and disposal will cause.

recyc

There is currently debate as to the relative efficiency and
administrative effectiveness of effluent charges (a tax upon wastes
that are discharged) and government regulations or standards
(absolute limits upon amounts that may be discharged).   The
principle that "the polluter pays" appeals to industry research
groups such as the Committee for Economic Development (CED)
because the decision about how much to clean up and how much to
pay is left to management and can be a competitive decision.
But when there is need to stop a waste (such as DDT or mercury)
that is detrimental if any more accumulates, then regulation is
needed. If a decrease will suffice or if you only need to minimize
a waste, then a tax will do. (See Marc Roberts, "On Reforming
Economic Growth," p. 127. "Readings")

A charge on effluents allows for economic adjustment using
the market-and-price mechanism. Pioneering work by economists
such as Allen Kneese and Edwin Mills shows how, if "social damage"
induced by pollution can be quantified, and if a means to assess a
tax for the amount of damage can be levied, then it is possible to
"internalize externalities" and the system will adjust to a more
environmentally responsible level.

Technological fixes are another way industry can protect the
environment at the manufacturing level. Pollution abatement
technology is a tech-fix. Recycling wastes is a tech-fix. (One
California power plant found that instead of discharging waste heat
into the environment as thermal pollution it could sell its low-grade
steam as an energy source for space-heating neighborhood homes.)
Recycling can be economically profitable as well as provide
environmental dividends. Environmentalists, however, maintain
that frequently tech-fixes, while solving one problem, may create
unanticipated and sometimes long-delayed side effects. (DDT is
the classic example.)

6.2.3
Consumer Adjustments

The consumer pays for the abatement
of industrial pollution through the higher
prices he pays for the product.

Question: How great will the consumer's cost be?

Question: How is this cost allocated among consumers? Is this cost
like a sales tax and regressive? (Where an "externality is
internalized" and passed on to the consumer as an increase in
price, it will function like a sales tax and be regressive -- but
tend to reduce demand. Where the cost of abatement is paid for
out of government revenues raised by progressive rather than
regressive taxes, it will not function like a sales tax or reduce
demand. Where the abatement is a design standard -- auto
emission standards, for example -- the equipment cost increases
perhaps but there is no regressive effluent tax on gasoline.)

Rationing at the consumer level could be used in the case of
energy or resource scarcity to limit use ("demand"). It could also
be used to limit environmental pollution. (See "Environmental Impact:
Controlling the Overall Level," by Westman and Gifford, and
"Gasoline Rationing as a Solution to Resource. Environmental and
Urban Problems," by Musial and Stearns. "Readings")

6.2.4
Governmental Adjustments

The SCEP report summarizes "the means available within the
political process and legal system . . . include taxes designed as
incentives, stimuli, or pressures; regulations, typically involving
a statute, an administrative agency, and supplementary action
through the courts; common-law remedies in the courts, incrementally
adjusted to contemporary needs; governmental financing of research
and assistance to facilitate costly adjustments to desired changes;
and governmental operations, civilian and military. Governmental
action in its own house can have a dual importance: in itself and as
a model for others to follow." (p. 34)

SCEP recommends as a point of departure for taking action
a principle of presumptive "source" responsibility.
"While remedial measures can be attempted on the routes along
which pollutants spread or in the reservoirs in which they accumulate,
we believe that these measures should be generally taken at the 'sources,
which we define broadly to include
(1) sources
or the points in the processess of production,
distribution, and consumption,
at which the pollutant is generated,
for example, factories, power plants,
stockyards, bus lines;
(2) proto sources
or earlier points that set the conditions
leading to the emission of pollutants
at a later stage,
for example, the manufacturers of
automobiles that emit pollutants
when driven by motorists,
or the brewers of beer sold
in nonreturnable cans
that are tossed aside
by the consumer;
and (3) secondary sources
or points along the routes
where pollutants are
concentrated
before moving on
to the reservoirs,
for example,
sewage treatment plants
or solid waste
disposal centers." (p. 33)

7.
Adjustments in Our Thinking

7.1
From "Isolated Problems" to "Holistic Thinking"

Our environmental problem is not a series of isolated
problems, each of which we can attempt to solve in turn. From
wellhead or mine all the way to the dump we need to change our
thinking so that we think holistically and see ourselves as participants
functioning within the great systems of our natural environment.

We need both to perceive these great systems and to understand them. When we understand them, we will be concerned about our poisoning them, clogging them, damaging them or modifying them with effects we don't yet see clearly.

<u>Question:</u> How do we educate those who are not biologists to perceive and to understand the systemic character of our natural environment? Who needs to grasp these things? Certainly engineers, economists, political leaders, all of whom make decisions affecting our natural environment. The P.E.E.M. project at M.I.T. issued in December 1974 an important summary of <u>Resource Materials for Professional Education in Environmental Management.</u> (See "Readings.") Among the resource materials included are those concerned with "conceptual approach to professional education in environmental management" and also "outlines and bibliographies for subject areas in environmental management."

In our more rural past the general public lived closer to the natural cycles and had an intuitive grasp of the systemic character of our natural environment. This intuitive sense has weakened or gone -- and needs to be revived. For example, one of the great natural cycles that we have interrupted looks like this:

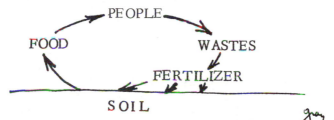

Instead we have taken human wastes and put them into the water cycle, which has resulted not only in an over-abundance of nutrients in the water cycle but also a hole in the food cycle because the natural fertilizer (our human waste) was going in the water rather than onto the land.

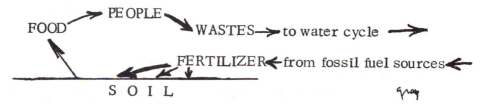

In place of the natural fertilizer we have substituted chemical fertilizers derived in substantial part from fossil fuel sources -- at the expense of our energy reserves. (See "Illinois Earth" and "Lake Erie," chapters 5 and 6 in <u>The Closing Circle: Nature, Man, and Technology,</u> by Barry Commoner. See also "Oil in Your Corn," <u>Wall Street Journal,</u> Nov. 11, 1973. "Readings")

In this example the costs of misplaced wastes were two-fold: there were the environmental costs to the waterways and those who used them, and there were the energy-availability costs. We paid both ways because in making our policies we were not thinking holistically, and isolated decision-makers dealt separately with a series of isolated problems.

7.2
From "Limits" to "Givens"

We still tend to think about the environment in terms of limits: "How far can we go before we reach critical points, clog systems, overload circuits?" This is an important and necessary way to think while we are being forced to adjust our environmental responses to environmental limits. But even while we do this, we may ask ourselves

Question: Is thinking about the environment in terms of "limits" the most helpful longer-term way for us to think about our environmental life-support systems?

We need to recognize that environmental limits aren't simply physical limits but they involve a somewhat different sort of limit, system limits. Physical limits are frequently like sports records; with skill, diligence, and perhaps luck you may find a way to penetrate a physical limit. For a long time we thought the sound barrier was an impenetrable physical limit.

When we press against or through physical limits in a system, the system to a point is resiliant and -- within system limits -- accommodates, although system functioning is usually somewhat impaired. (Your body temperature is an example of such a system.)

Beyond certain definite system limits, however, a threshold is reached. Thereafter system resiliancy diminishes very rapidly. (Your system for body-temperature control does not self-correct above about 107° or below about 89°. The "normal" limits are a narrow range of plus or minus 1° around 98.6°. When you are "running a temperature" you break these usual physical barriers but not the system limits. When you break the system limits, death results.)

We need to stop thinking of environmental limits as somehow like the sound barrier. Human society is not a supersonic jet that, when properly designed, can crash through these environmental limits on its trajectory through time.

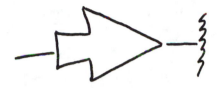

Instead we need to think of environmental limits as system limits, not merely physical limits. The environment is an enfolding context or system of "givens" -- akin to the structure of twenty-four hours in a day. We can sleep a little more or a little less, but there is no living way we escape this structure, nor do we need to in order to "do our thing."

Question: Do we not, as a matter of fact, have to redo our culture's whole sense of what "limits" mean?

Limits are perceived in our culture as negative, as a challenge to our inventive technology and to our human will. Limits are to be broken, overcome, surpassed. If the biosphere really is the life-support system of the "spaceship Earth," then the experience of our astronauts becomes a parable: Life-support systems are not challenges to be broken or exceeded, but they are instead vital "givens," essential parameters of existence within which we accomplish our human purposes. (See the discussion of limits in "The Human Dimensions of Limiting Growth," by David Dodson Gray. Also "Masculine Consciousness and the Problem of Limiting Growth," by Elizabeth Dodson Gray. "Readings" for the "Consciousness" section.)

SELECTED READINGS

Overview

Commoner, Barry, "The Ecosphere" from The Closing Circle:
Nature, Man and Technology. New York: Alfred Knopf, Inc.,
1971.

Lovins, Amory, "Long-Term Constraints on Human Activity" in
Growth and Its Implications for the Future, Vol. 2. Washington:
Government Printing Office, 1974.

Global Problems

Report of the Study of Critical Environmental Problems (SCEP).
Cambridge, Mass.: M.I.T. Press, 1970.

Report of the Study of Man's Impact on Climate (SMIC).
Cambridge, Mass.: M.I.T. Press, 1971.

Principles for Evaluating Chemicals in the Environment.
Washington, D.C.: National Academy of Sciences, 1975.

Assessing Potential Ocean Pollutants. Washington, D.C.: National
Academy of Sciences, 1975.

Environmental Impact

Clark, Lindley H., Jr., "Oil in Your Corn." Wall Street Journal,
November 13, 1973.

Hardin, Garrett, "Guilty Until Proven Innocent" in Exploring New
Ethics for Survival. New York: Viking Press, 1972.

Adjustment Proposals

Gray, Elizabeth Dodson, "Psycho-Sexual Roots of Our Ecological
Crisis." Unpublished paper, 1975.

"More Effective Programs for a Cleaner Environment," A Statement
on National Policy by the Research and Policy Committee of
the Committee for Economic Development (CED), April 1974.

Matthews, William H., Resource Materials for Professional Education
in Environmental Management. Unpublished Technical Report
prepared for the United Nations Environment Programme, 1974.

4

POPULATION, FOOD AND LAND

"There were a billion people in 1850,

when the Crimean War was brewing up.

There were 2 billion when Wall Street crashed in 1929,

and 3 billion in 1960 when Kennedy first went to the White House.

We shall reach the 4 billion mark around 1975." (Jon Tinker)

These figures suggest disturbing questions about

how all these people will eat,

and where and how they will live.

The recent drought and famine in sub-Saharan Africa

and in India

have made the predictions by world food experts

of a severe food shortage for the entire planet

seem more real.

POPULATION, FOOD, AND LAND

SUMMARY

1. The Interlocking Chain

2. What Are The Facts?

    2.1 Population Data -- U.S.
    2.2 Population Data -- World
    2.3 U.S. Agriculture and the World's Food Needs
    2.4 Man's Abuse of the Soil

3. Where Are The Limits?

    3.1 Area Under Cultivation as a Limit
    3.2 Can Technology Increase the Crop-Yield per acre?
    3.3 We Could Grow More Food, But . . .

4. The Shift from Grain to Animal Proteins in Affluent Countries

5. Policy Questions Confronting the United States

    5.1 "Upstairs, Downstairs" on a Global Level
    5.2 Policy Choices Now
    5.3 In Our Own Back Yard: Domestic Land-Use Issues

1.
The Interlocking Chain

Population, food and land are tied together like an interlocking chain. Like the rings of a Chinese puzzle, these three aspects of human existence just won't come apart no matter how we tug and pull. What is a problem in one sector is quickly felt in the others, too often with disastrous results.

We can describe the vicious-circle process by a litany:

> More people
>> means more food is needed.
>
> More food
>> means more land is needed.
>> Or more intensive agricultural practices.
>
> But more intensive agricultural practices
>> deplete the land more quickly.
>
> So soon there is less food,
>> more people eat less,
>
> And so on and on.

"More people" has also, for a number of reasons, meant more urbanization, and this has often used for other purposes land that had been agricultural land.

Lester R. Brown has written about the way in which "trends of expanding food production and growing population have reinforced each other." "Technological advances in agriculture and consequent increases in food supply have permitted population to increase. Population increases in turn generate pressure for agricultural innovation. . . . Population growth continues to absorb all the great increases in food production in the great majority of poor countries."

* "Population and Affluence: Growing Pressures on World Food Resources," p. 6. See "Readings.")

2.
<u>What Are The Facts?</u>

In considering population, food and land problems   population seems to be the supercharger, the one that is pushing the others around and around again.

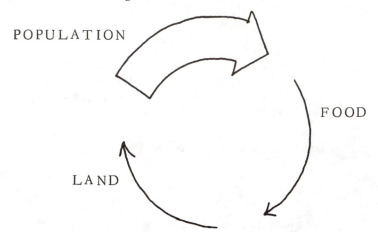

POPULATION

FOOD

LAND

So let us first examine the data about population in the United States and the world.

2.1
<u>Population Data -- U.S.</u>

The U.S. Bureau of the Census presents us with some encouraging population information, namely a significant decline in fertility rate since 1960.   The 1971 rate was nearly 31% lower than the 1960 rate.   But fertility rate per woman will need to remain at this zero population growth (ZPG) level for about seventy-five years before the total population size actually stops growing. All the girls already born who have not yet reached child-bearing age are the reason for this time lag.

> The ZPG concept is commonly misunderstood. . . .
> Attainment of the ZPG fertility rate does not mean that
> the population has stopped growing. What it does mean
> is that the rate, if maintained consistently over a long
> enough time, would ultimately cause the population to
> stop growing.*

---

* *The Use of Land: A Citizens' Policy Guide to Urban Growth,* A Task Force Report
Sponsored by the Rockefeller Brothers Fund, 1973, p. 77. See "Readings."

2.2
Population Data -- World

While U.S. data may give some grounds for hope, the worldwide figures can only be characterized as grim. World population is expected to arrive at 4 billion in 1975 and, if world population trends continue, to approach 7 billion by the end of this century.* This increase in world population by billions is a chilling example of exponential growth.

It took us 79 years to grow from 1 to 2 billion (1850-1929), only 31 years to grow from 2 to 3 billion (1929-1960), and now only 15 years to go from 3 to 4 billion in 1975. **

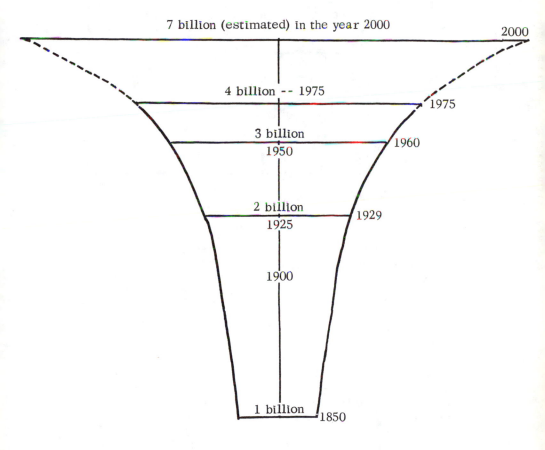

7 billion (estimated) in the year 2000

2000

4 billion -- 1975

1975

3 billion

1950

1960

2 billion

1925

1929

1900

1 billion

1850

* "World Population: U.N. on the Move but Grounds of Optimism Are Scant," by Constance Holden. *Science,* March 1974. See "Readings."

** "Whose Baby Is Population Control?" by Jon Tinker. *New Scientist,* Feb. 28, 1974. See "Readings."

The population of developing countries (where malnutrition afflicts 60% of the population and half have not yet reached reproductive years) will double in a generation at current fertility rates. William F. Draper, a world-population activist, is cited by Holden as summing up the dire projections in these words:

> We're at a point in history that's never even been dreamed of before. It's just going to engulf the world.

Given a population supercharger of these proportions, where do we stand with the interlocking problems of food and land?

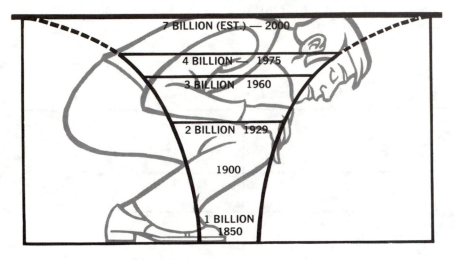

2.3
U.S. Agriculture and the World's Food Needs

Lester R. Brown says that "Over the past generation the U.S. has achieved a unique position as a supplier of food to the rest of the world." Prior to World War II the countries of Latin America, especially Argentina, were major grain exporters. Since then a combination of increasing populations and a lack of modernization of their agriculture have transformed the countries of Latin America from exporters to net importers of food. The United States and Canada have emerged in the last thirty years as the breadbaskets of the world.*

During this period U.S. policy was to intervene whenever famine threatened anywhere in the world. The world had two major food reserves: the reserves of grain in the leading exporting countries and cropland idled by government policy in the U.S. But in the late 1960s this buffer of idle land and grain reserves decreased in size. By 1973 it was no longer a buffer against food shortfalls and volatile prices.

* "Population and Affluence," pp. 16-17.

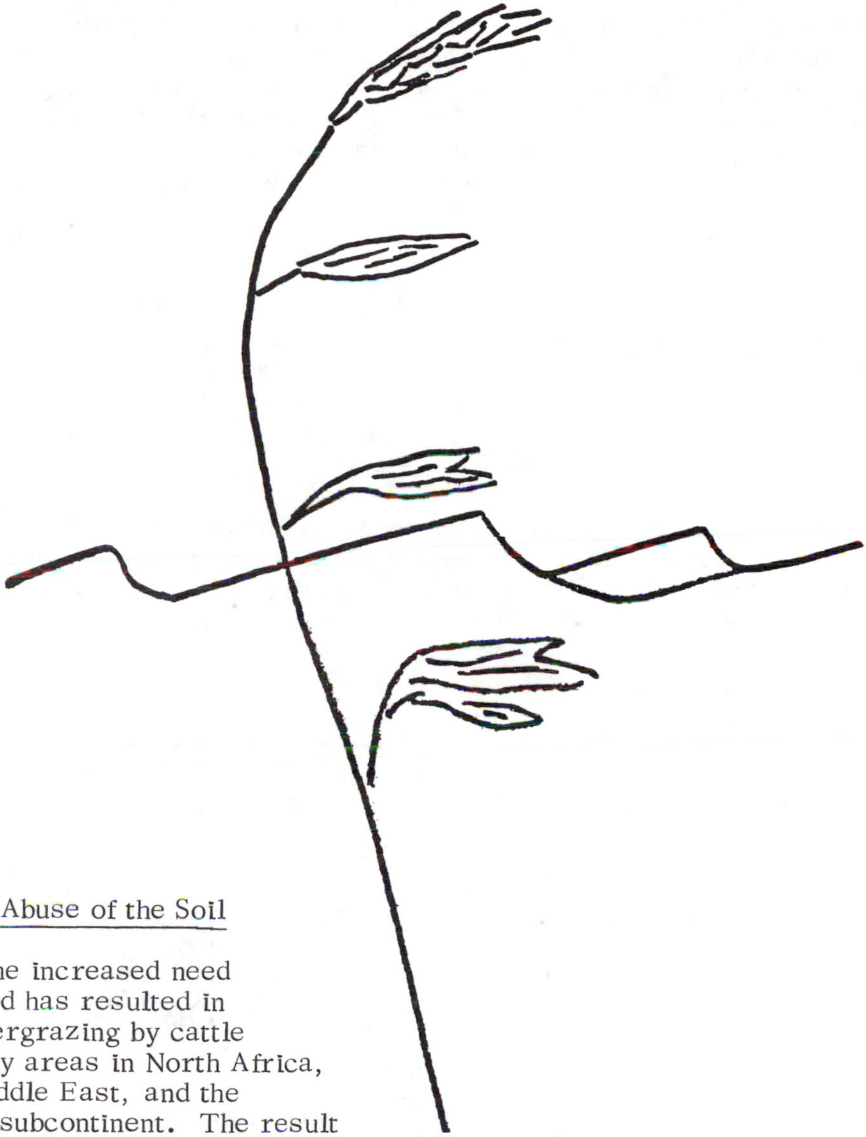

2.4
Man's Abuse of the Soil

The increased need
for food has resulted in
the overgrazing by cattle
of many areas in North Africa,
the Middle East, and the
Indian subcontinent. The result
is that the land is stripped of its
precious topsoil. The increased
need for agricultural land and
for wood for fuel has denuded
many areas of trees.   This has
resulted in serious erosion.
Millions of acres of denuded land are abandoned each year to winds
and rains, and their rural populations are forced to seek a life in
the overcrowded cities.

As the demand for food increases, more and more marginal land is brought under cultivation. As farmers plant further up on hillsides, there is further erosion and often (as in West Pakistan) the eroded soil is not only stripped from hillside fields but silts up behind the irrigation dams in the valleys. Lester Brown cites as a historic example of the effects of man's abuse of the soil "North Africa, once the fertile granary of the Roman Empire and now largely a desert or near-desert whose people are fed with the aid of food imports from the U.S. Once-productive land was eroded by continuous cropping and overgrazing until much of it would no longer sustain agriculture. Irrigation systems silted, depriving land of the water needed for cultivation."*

3.
Where Are The Limits?

3.1
Area Under Cultivation as a Limit

The food supply can be expanded by increasing the area under cultivation. This was the intention of the virgin-lands project in the late 1950s in which 100 million acres of dry land in the Soviet Union were plowed up, only to find they were too dry to grow a crop every year.

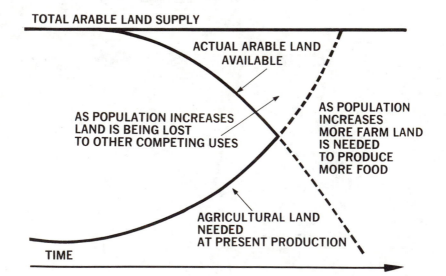

*Lester Brown, "Population and Affluence," p. 14.

It is difficult to expand the area under cultivation in the developed countries. In Japan and Western Europe there has been a decline in land used for crop production. In the U.S. farmland has been taken for other purposes, especially for suburban housing, without regard for its unique food-bearing capacity as farmland. In most countries there are no well-defined land-use policies protecting agricultural land from other uses. (See the Rockefeller Land Use report. "Readings.")

Large areas of agricultural land are being lost to erosion by wind or water in the Middle East, the Indian subcontinent, the Caribbean, North Africa, Central America, and the Andean countries of South America. Limits to the amount of water available for irrigation also limit the amount of area that can be cultivated. *

All this is a fleshing out in gruesome detail and living color of what is involved as one of the major parameters in the Limits to Growth model:

> There has been an overwhelming excess of potentially arable land for all of history, and now, within 30 years (or about one population doubling time), there may be a sudden and serious shortage. Like the owner of the lily pond in (Limits) chapter I, the human race may have very little time to react to a crisis resulting from exponential growth in finite space. **

Question: Is the quantity of arable land a limit to food and population? How close to that limit are we today?

Question: How feasible are technologies for growing food without land? (The ocean is obviously one -- but we seem to have neared the limit in increase from that source. Are there other non-land ways to grow food?)

3.2
Can Technology Increase the Crop-Yield per acre?

The alternative to the area-expanding method of increasing crop yields has been to increase the crop yield from each acre. The Green Revolution that has accounted for 4/5th of the annual increase in world food output during the early 1970s*** was a technological "fix" of truly massive proportions.

* Lester Brown, "Population and Affluence," p. 14.

** *Limits,* p. 51

*** Lester Brown, p. 6

At the global level the record of the past two decades suggests it is far cheaper and easier to expand the food supply by intensifying cultivation of the existing cropland than by bringing new land under the plow.*

Question: How can existing cropland be protected as an essential food-and-population input from encroachments of other uses and other technologies?

Question: What can be done to help the agricultural system compete with other sectors for needed inputs? Will the market-and-price mechanism and the profit incentive be sufficient?

The Green Revolution is a "tech fix," not a solution. It is a means of buying time so that an attempt can be made to curb population growth. And even as a "tech fix," it has had its limiting side-effects. Anthony Lewis reports an interview with Prof. Nevin Scrimshaw of M.I.T.'s Dept. of Nutrition and Food Science: "Even better strains of plants need well-watered land, and water is limited. Then if your population and affluence begin to swallow up the gain . . . "**

Another limit of the Green Revolution is the stresses on the environment that come with technological agriculture. Eutrophication of lakes comes from nitrogen runoff from fertilizer into streams. The irrigation-induced "snail fever" today afflicts 1 out of 14 of those alive. The silting of lakes behind great irrigation dams like the Egyptian Aswan dam will greatly shorten the useful life of the dams and the irrigation projects that depend upon them. The Aswan dam also removed from downstream farmlands the annual deposit of fertilizing nutrients that used to be left behind by the annual floods now "brought under control."

Question: What is the likelihood of new technologies that could alleviate undesirable side effects of any of the six major technological advances Lester Brown cites?

Question: What is the likelihood of new technologies increasing the per/acre yield of soybeans? (This single breakthrough would be most helpful in increasing the world protein supply.)

Another cost of the Green Revolution is the increased potential

* Lester Brown, "Population and Affluence," p. 8

** "Nearing the Limits," *New York Times,* Oct. 1, 1973

for instability in crop yields. Monoculture agriculture in which vast
acreages are sown in a single variety of high-yield/acre crop are
much more vulnerable to disaster when a disease strikes than
was the case when the land was planted in a number of varieties
or a number of crops. Likewise crops protected by DDT remove
not only pests but predators, so that when a new pest that is more
resistent to DDT appears there are no predators.

Certainly the over-fishing of our oceans and the resource-
inspired conflicts among national fishing fleets must also be reckoned
on the "cost" side of our efforts to get more food.

The new farming and cattle-fattening technologies have produced
food of increasingly questionable consequences for long-term health.
Pesticides on fruit, carcinogens in meat, preservatives and additives
in processed food -- all suggest a newly emerging health hazard of
as-yet-unknown proportions.

3.3
We Could Grow More Food, But . . .

The systemic nature of our problem in growing more food is
illustrated by an article in the Wall Street Journal (March 11, 1974).*
There was concern in the spring of 1974 that farmers might be
unmotivated to try to surpass the record crops of 1973 because of
rising prices of everything farmers need from seed and fertilizer
through to farm equipment and baling wire. In addition to these
rising prices (and fueling them) were serious shortages in all these
areas.

"Why can't the farmer substitute something else for what's in
short supply?" You learn it is a complicated story of how there is
a problem in everything else too. Then add in the time factor.
Crops need to be planted in order to get growing -- or they won't be
planted at all. Many of these shortages "seem to come up out of
nowhere," as one man put it. There is also the time it takes for new
producers of fertilizer to get into production.

You get a picture of a whole interconnected story. The end result
is that farmers perceive that more work this year may earn them less
money than last year. So will they bother to grow more? Would you?

Question: What sorts of production-oriented incentives are there
        besides profit?

* See "Readings."

Question: How can farmers be encouraged to plant maximum acreage? Is the need for world food reserves sufficient for the U.S. to insulate farmers from the market risks of shifts in demand? Do the Commodity Markets do this sufficiently?

DAYS OF WORLD GRAIN CONSUMPTION

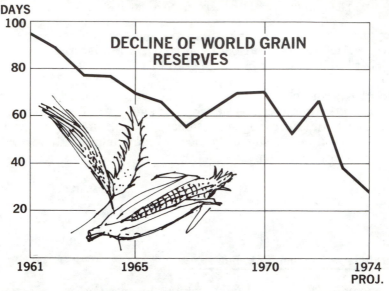

The fossil-fuel energy required for present high-technology agriculture suggests that there will be still another limit to food production if (when) we return to an exclusively solar-powered agriculture without fossil-fuel inputs.

Prior to gasoline-powered tractors and artificial fertilizers based upon natural-gas molecules, American farmers used horse-drawn equipment, organic fertilizers, and let land lay fallow in a nitrogen-fixing cover crop which later was plowed under to enrich the soil. Solar energy rather than fossil-fuels powered and fertilized the farm.

But prior to fossil-fuels only one-third of the arable land was available each year to produce the current crop. Another third was in forage, growing feed for the horses, and the final third lay fallow each year. The switch to fossil fuels for power and fertilizer had the effect of increasing available arable land for effective annual use by 300%.

Question: What would be the effect of returning to solar-powered agriculture (without fossil-fuel inputs) upon the amount of available arable land annually in cash-crop use?

Question: What other systemic effects would follow from a return to solar-powered agriculture, in addition to the effect upon agricultural output?

4.

The Shift from Grain to Animal Proteins in Affluent Countries

The world food picture was bad, but it is being further exacerbated by changes in the affluence (and hence the diets) of residents of the industrialized "Northern tier" countries -- the United Kingdom, Scandinavia, Western Europe, Eastern Europe, Russia, Japan, Canada and the United States.

The world food problem was perceived in the 1960s as a nip and tuck race between population growth and food supplies. In the 1970s it has become clear that this already tight race between food and population-growth is being further complicated by affluence-induced changes in eating patterns of the rich. Grain that could have fed ten poor people in developing countries can now be profitably fed to cattle to provide beef to feed one affluent person in a Northern-tier industrial country. If he or she can get it, a poor person in a developing country will consume about 400 pounds of grain a year; in the U.S. one person consumes 2000 pounds a year -- 150 pounds directly in bread and cereal, the rest in the form of meat, eggs and dairy products.

> The agricultural resources -- land, water, fertilizer -- required to support an average North American are nearly five times those of the average Indian, Nigerian, or Colombian. (Lester Brown, "Population and Affluence," p. 3)

We must now revise our "litany" describing the vicious-circle process by which population-growth supercharges pressures upon food and thereby pressure upon land. It must be revised to begin

> More people
> require more food.
> But rich people
> require much more food. . . .

Question: What is the likelihood of technologies shifting consumer food habits from animal proteins toward vegetable proteins?

5.
Policy Questions Confronting the United States

5.1
"Upstairs, Downstairs" on a Global Level

Jon Tinker, writing before the World Population Conference in Bucharest, Roumania, in August 1974, observed*

> One issue which the developing countries will undoubtedly press is that of population control in the rich, white, northern nations.
> While the physical pressure of human numbers is greatest in the poor countries, it is the rich nations which consume disproportionate quantities of food and raw materials. There is much justification for the view that one extra American is a worse disaster for the world than a dozen extra Asians.

* John Tinker, "Whose Baby Is Population Control?" *New Scientist,* Feb. 28, 1974.

It all begins to feel like an evening with the TV drama series "Upstairs, Downstairs," about an Edwardian English household of wealth and servant-classes. But now the "Upstairs, Downstairs" isn't Edwardian but present-day, and it is a global household we are thinking about.

Question: Will "downstairs" quietly starve while watching "upstairs" eat meat? (Would you?)

Question: What happens as human beings to "upstairs" as they watch TV during dinner and see "downstairs" starving?

During the World Food Conference at Rome in the fall of 1974 the following cartoon appeared, suggesting a comparison with the great feast of a Biblical oppressor, King Belshazzar (Daniel 5). It is from that Biblical account that we get our saying about "seeing the handwriting on the wall." The original words that were written were Mene (God has measured your sovereignty and put an end to it) and Tekel (You have been weighed in the balance and found wanting).

Behrendt (Reprinted by permission of Rothco)

MENE TEKEL.....

<u>Question:</u> If you were downstairs and hungry, wouldn't you at least enjoy sex and your children?

<u>Question:</u> What would be the effect upon the world food and population prospects if the affluent were to alter consumption patterns back from animal protein to vegetable protein, just as we already have gone from animal fats (butter and lard) to vegetable oils (oleo and Crisco)?

<u>Question:</u> A low-chloresterol diet is low in animal fats. What health dividends might be expected in terms of reduced health hazards, if affluent populations shifted from animal proteins toward vegetable proteins? Less heart disease? Less cancer? (See "Readings.")

5.2
<u>Policy Choices Now</u>

Richard Critchfield, writing in the <u>Christian Science Monitor</u>, summarizes the current situation like this:

One-fourth of the world is losing its fight to survive. What will America do about it? Normally restrained experts on energy, agriculture, population, and the global economy are starting to predict bankruptcy, social breakdown, and starvation for as many as 1 billion people by late this year or early 1975.

Some thirty countries could be affected, mostly in tropical Africa, South Asia, and the Central American-Caribbean area. When one adds everything together -- more floods, more drought at a time of low world food reserves, bankrupt countries unable to import enough food to feed their growing cities nor enough fertilizer to grow (food) in the countryside, populations reaching critical densities -- it is hard to see anything immediately ahead save one violent political explosion after another. (Mar. 7, 1974)

A "Marshall Plan" for food to aid the developing nations was proposed at the April 1974 Special Session of the UN General Assembly. "Fourth World" nations -- nations without significant mineral or commodity resources -- asked for special help from Western countries, Japan, the Soviet Union, and the affluent Arab countries of the "upstairs" portion of the old Third World bloc.

<u>Question:</u> What leadership can the U.S. effectively take? Would a "Marshall Plan" for food help? Or would it only save more people who would then increase their numbers?

"What I'm trying to say is we're all in this thing together."

<u>Question</u>: Is it possible for the U.S. to pursue an isolationist
policy about world food and world population? Would that
be expedient over the long run?

<u>Question</u>: Can the U.S. exist politically in a world struggling
with social unrest of these dimensions? Can it exist economically?
How may such unrest affect the U.S.?

<u>Question</u>: If the U.S. does nothing now, will we face "triage" choices
later? Or are we already facing them now? (See the article by
the Paddocks in the "Readings.")   What are the ethical dimensions
of such "triage" choices?

<u>Question</u>: How do domestic land-use and energy policies affect
the world food-response capabilities of the U.S.?

<u>Question</u>: Has the U.S. a policy about malnutrition in the U.S.?
Is domestic malnutrition a part of (or different from) the
world food problem?

<u>Question</u>: What should be the response of the U.S. and other
affluent countries to the proposal from developing countries
that population control should be pressed in affluent countries
because of the greater resource pressure from affluent citizens?
Does the U.S. need a national ZPG goal and accompanying policies
and programs?

5.3
In Our Own Back Yard: Domestic Land-Use Issues

The Use of Land is billed as "A Citizens' Policy Guide to Urban Growth." It is a Task Force report sponsored by the Rockefeller Brothers Fund, and is concerned to balance two needs:

--the need to protect the environmental, cultural, and aesthetic characteristics of the land

and

--the need to provide facilities for the future growth in the U.S. population. (From now until 1985 more than 27,000 new households will be formed each week.)

The Rockefeller Land Use report notes that, because of our national history, our laws and institutions have a pro-development bias. Consequently we have neither "adequate institutional processes nor the necessary legal doctrine to solve the problems of urban growth." (p. 15)

The report recommends that the States (not individual localities) "must have the responsibility to control land-use decisions that affect the interests of people beyond local boundaries if critical environmental lands are to be protected and if development needed by a regional population is not to be blocked by local governments." (p. 15)

The report attempts to focus on "positive inducements" rather than "negative compulsion," and tries to find a balance between environmental needs and development needs of society. Both the regulation of development and incentives for better development are proposed.

Certain legal changes are proposed: (a) that the "courts should presume that any change in existing natural ecosystems is likely to have adverse consequences -- therefore the proponent of the change be required to prep   environmental impact statement." (p. 174) (b) that the Supreme Court reexamine its precedents on the "taking issue" and "seek to balance public benefit against land value lost," with the awareness that U.S. constitutional doctrine was formulated when "land was regarded as unlimited and its use not ordinarily of concern to society." (p. 174)

Question: Is the Rockefeller report correct? Do we need to balance our environmental and development needs?

Question: Is the State the proper locus of regulatory authority in the cases cited?

Question: Is it likely or feasible that our legal doctrine will change to allow for public-interest regulation of the development of private land for profit?

Question: Are there alternative means by which urban sprawl and chaotic growth can be stemmed?

Question: Should agricultural land in the United States be protected for agricultural use? What relationships are there between global population-food issues and our domestic land-use policies?

Question: The continued availability of natural gas and petroleum affects our sense of how much arable land we can spare for other uses. How scarce would we judge arable land to be (and how much could be spared for other uses) if our agriculture were to have to become once again entirely solar-powered in ten or twenty-five years?

Question: Have we adequately assessed the land we will need in order to grow sufficient food for ourselves and for other parts of the world?

SELECTED READINGS

Population Growth

Holden, Constance, "World Population: U.N. on the Move but Grounds for Optimism are Scant." Science, Mar. 1, 1974.

Tinker, Jon, "Whose Baby Is Population Control?" New Scientist, Feb. 28, 1974.

Food and Population System

Brown, Lester R., "Population and Affluence: Growing Pressures on World Food Reserves." Population Bulletin, Vol. 29, No. 2.

Foreign Policy special section, "An Exchange on Food" between Charles G. Billo and Lester R. Brown. Spring 1974.

Spurgeon, David, "The Nutrition Crunch: A World View." Science and Public Affairs, October 1973.

Food and Population Policy for the U.S. in the World

Paddock, William and Paul, "Herewith Is a Proposal for the Use of American Food: 'Triage' " in Famine 1975!: America's Decision -- Who Will Survive? Boston: Little, Brown and Co., 1967.

Hardin, Garrett, "Lifeboat Ethics: The Case Against Helping the Poor" in Psychology Today, September 1974.

Faramelli, Norman J., "Lifeboat Ethics: Or the Case for Genocide by Benign Neglect" in Church and Society, March-April 1975.

Domestic Land-Use Policy

Cahn, Robert, "Where Do We Grow From Here?" The Christian Science Monitor, May 1973.

The Use of Land: A Citizens' Policy Guide to Urban Growth, A Task Force Report Sponsored by the Rockefeller Brothers Fund. New York: Thomas Y. Crowell, 1973. Selected chapters.

5

ECONOMIC GROWTH -- HOW MUCH AND HOW?

Critics of growth suggest that we must limit economic growth

before we use up our resources

and permanently damage our environment.

On the other hand,

as even small recessions let us know,

we seem dependent upon economic growth for jobs

and for our standard of living.

Are we "locked into" two irreconcilable positions?

Will we march off that environmental cliff

affluently clutching our two-cars-in-every-garage

and a chicken-in-every-pot?

Or will we stop our economic growth too soon

and with great social cost,

needlessly frightened by environmental Cassandras?

Or is there some other way?

HOW BIG IS BEST?

ECONOMIC GROWTH -- HOW MUCH AND HOW?

SUMMARY

1. Look at the Whole System: Issues

2. Beyond the Pros and Cons: The Debate

3. Resource Shortages and Economic Growth

4. The Environmental Costs and Economic Growth

5. Costs and Benefits to Society of Economic Growth
   and No-Growth

1.
Look at the Whole System: Issues

Question: Can we continue to grow while (1) preserving the health
   of our environment, and (2) not seriously depleting our
   resources?

Question: What are the constraints upon economic growth posed
   by our biological life-support system -- in particular, what
   are the constraints upon growth of the use of energy and
   materials?   What are the constraints upon growth from our
   outputs of environmental pollutants? Do these constraints
   compel a necessary maximum limit to economic activity?

Question: What are the constraints which our economy and social
   system pose -- such as "acceptable" employment levels and
   inflation rates, accustomed standards of living, and adequate
   military security?   Do these constraints compel a necessary
   minimum limit to economic activity?

Question: How can we balance the fragilities of our economic and
   social system with the fragilities of our natural environment?

Question: Given these constraints, what is the minimum acceptable
   growth? What is the maximum?

2.
Beyond the Pros and Cons: The Debate

"Growth or No Growth, That Is Not the Relevant Question, "
Ronald Ridker writes in Science (December 28, 1973. See "Readings.")
The economist Walter Heller has written in a similar vein:
"A conference of ecologists and environmentalists, economists and
technologists -- convened to illuminate the complex interplay of
energy, economic growth, and the environment -- should open not
with a declaration of war or of conflicting faiths, but with a
declaration of humility."

The fact that energy, economics, and ecology are closely
related is now being recognized by many diverse people. (See,
for example, "Energy, Ecology, and Economics " by Howard T.
Odum of the Department of Environmental Engineering Services,
University of Florida. "Readings")   Energy, economics, and
ecology each provide constraints which affect the others. Equilibrium
in any one depends upon finding a balance of all three as systems
which, together, are the linchpins of the wheels that move our larger
social and physical life-support system.

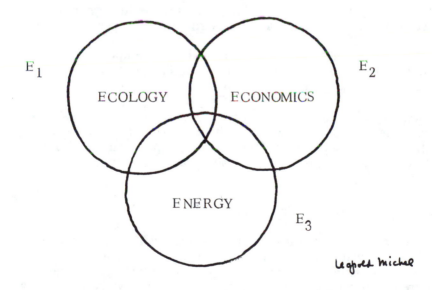

The Three E's are "Chain-linked."

As the argumentative spirit of opposing camps cools somewhat, perhaps the cooperation that is necessary may be forthcoming so that we can all find some less argumentative middle ground. The Harvard economist Marc Roberts, writing "On Reforming Economic Growth" (Daedelus, Fall 1973. "Readings"), points us all toward this middle ground when he asks such questions as

Question: Can we maintain (economic) growth while minimizing use of certain resource inputs?

Question: Can we produce a constant output with a smaller flow of physical input?

Question: Can we maintain growth while lowering the output of various polluting materials?

Marc Roberts helps us all peek through the door to a room beyond the debate over Growth vs. No-Growth. What begins to emerge is a life system with a number of especially critical interacting components and constraints. Necessary follow-up questions about this more comprehensive life-system are these:

Question: In what respects is "economic growth" different from growth in quantity of physical outputs?

Question: If we were to decide to economize our use of resource and energy inputs over the longer term, could economic growth become in time less constrained by these economies?

Question: How long a time would be required to make these adjustments? How short a time could be required if this had to be done on a "crash" basis?

Question: What would be the likely effects of these changes upon inflation? Upon employment? Upon national defense? Upon the material standard of living? Upon the quality of life? Upon future availability of resource and energy inputs?

3.
Resource Shortages and Economic Growth

Resources for the Future, Inc., released a paper reviewing the year 1973. It was entitled "An Abundance of Shortages." Shortages were then occurring in nearly all sectors of the U.S. economy. Our experience with energy-shortages makes us aware that in addition to their direct effects such shortages have longer-term systemic effects that we do not yet perceive clearly.

Question: How well does our economic system adjust to shortages? Can this adjustment process be speeded?

Question: Will the market-and-price mechanism work now to
   spur new discoveries, new extraction technologies, and
   substitutes for resources in short supply? Why? Or why not?
   What "externalities" are generated by the working of the
   market mechanism? Under what conditions may the market-
   and-price mechanism not work? (See the sections on "The
   Marketplace" and "Technology."

Question: When energy is one of the critical resources in short
   supply, does this constrain our use of new technologies and
   substitutions as adjustment mechanisms?

Some economists are confident that the marketplace will
adjust both demand and supply. M. A. Adelman of M. I. T., for
example, asserts that there is no long-term energy crisis.
(See "Is the Oil Shortage Real?" in Foreign Policy, Winter 1972-3.
"Readings.") On the other hand, the director of the U.S. Geological
Survey, V. E. McKelvey, warns that only a few of our material
resource reserves will last well into the next century. (See
"Potential Mineral Reserves," in the "Readings" of the "Resources"
section.)

4.
Environmental Costs and Economic Growth

Economists once thought of our air and water resources as
"free goods." We now see that there are real costs to using the air
and water around us. They can be depleted or degraded like any
other resource.

As industry grew, pollution grew as well. Who should pay
for the environmental and social costs of pollution? How should
they be regulated? Economists such as Allen Kneese and Edwin
Mills are addressing themselves to the question of "internalizing
externalities." Herman Daly, Kenneth Boulding, Walter E.
Westman and Roger M. Gifford, among others, have addressed
themselves to the question of quotas, various forms of rationing,
and governmental regulation as ways of minimizing environmental
and social damage. (See "Readings" on "Adjustment Mechanisms.")

Still another facet of the growth debate as it affects the environment
is suggested by Tobin and Nordhaus at Yale, who have questioned
whether GNP is still an adequate indicator of economic growth benefits.
They have proposed a broader definition of "Net Economic Welfare"
in which social damage costs and the costs of their corrections are
deducted from GNP as costs of economic growth, rather than added
to GNP as though their correction somehow added to net economic
growth.

Question: Does the GNP concept need to be revised as a concept
   so that it expresses net (rather than gross) economic growth?

5.

Costs and Benefits to Society of Economic Growth and No-Growth

For a very long time the benefits of economic growth seemed clearly to outweigh its costs to us. Economic growth was an unquestioned good that gave us, among other things, longer lives, better nutrition, greater mobility, and an increasing material standard of living.

As we have become more sensitive to the mounting costs of economic growth to our society, we have had to realize that not only is our natural environment a fragile system but our social and economic life together is also a sensitive and fragile system. Stopping economic growth may relieve critical environmental costs but it may also cause other social costs. We may be trading one sort of externality for still another sort of externality.

A consideration of the externalities possibly resulting from slowing or stopping growth leads us to questions such as:

Question: Will a no-growth also be a no-population growth society?

Question: Under what conditions can a no-growth society provide employment for everyone?

Question: What can be expected to happen to the benefits of our past growth-society -- mobility, nutrition, life expectancy, material standard of living -- in a slower growing or no-growth society?

Question: In a slower growing or no-growth society what happens to the rising aspirations of the disadvantaged -- women, blacks, Chicanos, perhaps even the young? What other social catalysts can ease social conflict and facilitate social change as economic growth has done?

Question: Will a no-growth society be less concerned with fairness and economic justice, because improvements could no longer come out of "growth"? Or will a no-growth society be more concerned with fairness and economic justice, because societal cohesion demands less social and economic "distance" between top and bottom

Those who advocate continued economic growth must ask:

Question: What good to us will a rising material standard of living et al. be if our natural environment is polluted beyond safe levels?

Question: Can we learn to generate the economic growth we seek
without using (as we have in the past) ever greater resource inputs?

Question: Could our primary social benefits from growth be met
by an economy more oriented toward energy conservation and
increased product durability?

We are being driven, it seems to us, toward reform of our
economic system, so that its benefits continue or increase, and
the costs (resource, environmental, social) of those benefits are
better controlled.

SELECTED READINGS

The Case for No-Growth

Boulding, Kenneth, "The Economics of Spaceship Earth" (1964) in
Toward a Steady-State Economy, ed. Herman E. Daly.
San Francisco, Calif.: W. H. Freeman & Co., 1973.

Daly, Herman E., "The Steady-State Economy" (1971) in
Toward a Steady-State Economy.

Georgescu-Roegen, Nicholas, "The Entropy Law and the Economic
Problem" (1971) in Toward a Steady-State Economy.

The Case for Reforming Economic Growth

Ridker, Ronald G., "To Grow or Not to Grow: That's Not the
Relevant Question." Science, Dec. 28, 1973.

Roberts, Marc J., "On Reforming Economic Growth."
Daedelus, Fall 1973.

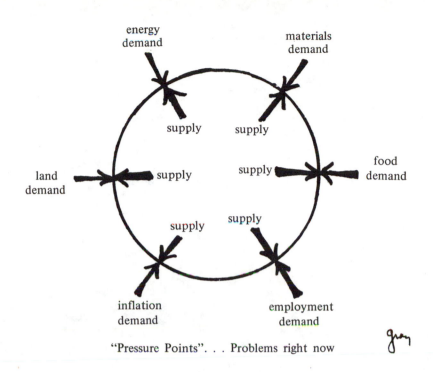

energy demand

materials demand

supply   supply

land demand   supply   supply   food demand

supply   supply

inflation demand   employment demand

"Pressure Points". . . Problems right now

PART 2

How Well Will
Our Adjustment Mechanisms Work?

6

MARKETPLACE ADJUSTMENT TO SCARCITY

Credit: Manpower

SUMMARY

1. Basic Issues

2. The Current Debate: The Market Mechanism and
    the Energy Crisis

3. Lessons from the Energy Crisis

    3.1 The Problem of Predicting Market Behavior
    3.2 The Problem of Social Resistance
    3.3 The Problem of Economic Justice and the Marketplace
    3.4 The Problem of Time Lags and the Marketplace

4. What Really Is Scarce?

5. The Profitability Limits of the Marketplace as
    an Adjustment Mechanism

6. Monopoly and Oligopoly Limits of Marketplace Adjustment
    to Scarcity

7. The Stability of Value of Financial Assets as
    a Marketplace Limit

8. Government Policy and the Marketplace

1.
Basic Issues

In last year's hearings about "Growth and Its Implications
for the Future," the following issues were included for consideration:

(1) To what extent can these market mechanisms be relied upon
to allocate resources and to buffer future generations from the rapid
decline depicted by Limits to Growth and Blueprint for Survival?

(2) What are the limitations of the marketplace? What additional
incentives and restraints would be required to supplement the price
system in order to influence the use and reuse of resources and to
influence the generation of pollutants?

(3) How can the marketplace influence research and development
efforts aimed at expanding the usability and reusability of resources
and at pollution control?

(4) What would be the impact of price determination by cartels
on the ability of the market to adjust consumption as physical limits
are approached?

2.
The Current Debate: The Market Mechanism and Energy Crisis

We have had the experience of the energy crisis since those earlier hearings.

<u>Question:</u> What have we learned from the energy crisis about the effectiveness and limitations of market behavior as an adjustment mechanism?

3.
Lessons from the Energy Crisis

3.1
The Problem of Predicting Market Behavior

The market-and-price mechanism responds very quickly to present imbalances of supply and demand. Short-term market behavior is easily understood. But who could have predicted five years ago (or one year ago) that the price of oil would triple in 1974? Or that Cadillacs would be a glut on the market?

<u>Question:</u> How effective is the market mechanism in anticipating <u>future</u> imbalances of supply and demand?

"Could we have guessed wrong somewhere?"

<u>Question</u>: Can the market-and-price mechanism anticipate long-
term scarcity by increasing prices in advance of scarcities?

There were things we could have done, given enough time,
that would have greatly eased the effect of the oil crisis. For
example, our homes and buildings could have been better insulated.
Our cars could have been smaller and more efficient. We could
have organized our cities and suburbs around a more energy-efficient
transportation system. But inexpensive energy was built into our
way of life so that it would be disruptive to make abrupt adjustments.

<u>Question</u>: If we are not going to get much hint of long-term market
and price behavior from the market, how do we prepare for
the future so that we can adjust our economic system and larger
social system smoothly?

<u>Question</u>: If we rely upon higher prices to motivate users to
economize and producers to increase capacity, can the marketplace still be relied upon to set those prices, or must those
prices be set in conjunction with another mechanism better
adapted to anticipating longer-term signals and to allowing for
non-market costs (political, social) of <u>not</u> adjusting the social
system smoothly?

"My whole life has been a shortfall."

Drawing by Stevenson; ©1973 The New Yorker Magazine, Inc.

3.2
The Problem of Social Resistance

When prices increase rapidly in response to scarcity, this
tends to do several things that generate social resistance by
people to the adjustments the marketplace normally would induce.
Often these social forces act to prohibit such adjustment.

For example, it was economically feasible at 1974 oil prices
to locate an oil refinery in New Hampshire to serve the New England
region.   But local government and townspeople agreed with
environmentalists in 1974 and have stopped the planned refinery.
The U.S. (and New England) probably needs more refineries, but
no one, at least in New England, wants the new refinery in their backyard.

On the demand (or users') side the strike over diesel-oil-price
increases in the winter of 1974 by a national coalition of groups of
independent truckers was also social resistance.   This time the
resistance wasn't expressed through political channels but through
direct social protest -- a refusal to continue to function, which had
the effect of a temper tantrum.   It was able to stop enough of the
rest of the system to get attention and quick action.

Market Price does not equal the Total Social Cost

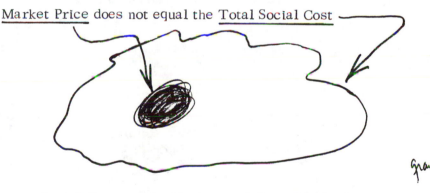

Social Costs of the Market-and-Price Mechanism

--Unemployment (from decreased demand)

--Inflation (higher prices)

--Social Unrest (conflict over access to the decreased supply)

examples to keep in mind:

                        --Irish Potato Famine of the 1840s
                        --Independent Truckers' Strike of 1974

101

Question: Is the market-and-price mechanism able to take into
consideration regional, environmental, and social resistance
by including these "social costs" in the eventual cost to the
consumer? Are these costs "externalities" that can be
"internalized"?

Question: To what extent is the market mechanism's reliance
upon profit to motivate behavior able (or unable) to cope with
certain forms of social resistance? With which forms is it
best able to cope? With which forms of social resistance is it
least able to cope?

Question: Are some social costs too great to be paid at any market
price? Can the marketplace make such a decision? Or
is that a decision that is made in some other way? How is it
decided?

3.3
The Problem of Economic Justice and the Marketplace

The assumption of market theory is that all participants in the
market have equal economic power so that price increases affect all
alike. When the price of oil rose so dramatically in the winter of
1973-74, the government attempted to control prices. M.I.T. economis
Paul MacAvoy argued that oil and gas prices should be deregulated.

"I'll tell you what's wrong. We're spending too much on necessities!"

This would have decreased demand and increased profit opportunities, and hence suppliers would have had additional motivation to increase supplies. However others argued that higher prices were like a regressive tax; the increase in price fell more heavily upon the poor because it used up proportionately much more of their income.

Question: Must we have an equal distribution of income for the market mechanism to function properly? To function equitably?

Question: Does an unequal distribution of income distort the functioning of the market mechanism?

Question: Does the functioning of the market mechanism place a disproportionate burden upon certain social and economic groups?

3.4
The Problem of Time-Lags and the Marketplace

Higher prices for energy tend to spur new discoveries on the supply side and new efficiencies and substitutions on the user or demand side. The crucial question is how long this will take. Oil men in Oklahoma and Texas are being encouraged to find oil by the new higher prices, but there are supply delays for them in getting their drilling equipment, let alone their locating new wells and getting the new oil to market.

Question: Is oil unique in that it takes a longer time for producers to increase supplies and for users to adjust to scarcity as signaled by higher oil prices? Or will we face these delays again with other resources?

Time-lags are the other end of a problem we indicated earlier -- the limitation of the market-and-price mechanism in anticipating future imbalances. Now we are looking at it from the point of view of the time it takes to adjust after the price and availability have changed.

4.
What Really Is Scarce?

A favorite argument of economists is that as the price increases to a profitable level for speculators, nothing remains scarce. Economists agree that there is a finite stock of each resource, but doubling the price makes it economic (profitable) to use less accessible or lower-grade reserves. Hence, they conclude, we will reach the end point of our reserves in the very distant future -- much later than Limits to Growth predicts. (See Wilfred Malenbaum, "Resource Shortages in an Expanding World." "Readings" in the "Resource Availability" section.)

Question: How does one contrast the economists' argument of almost infinite reserves with that of V. E. McKelvey, director of the U.S. Geological Survey, who argues that we are running out of many resources? (See "Potential Mineral Reserves" in the section on "Resource Availability.")

David Dodson Gray in his essay "Limitations of the Marketplace" (see "Readings") has raised the question of how the market-and-price mechanism functions in the limiting condition -- when a doubling or tripling in price will not increase supply because there is no way to increase supply.

Question: What happens when a price increase will not increase the supply because there is no more -- at all? (Does the market-and-price mechanism function in the same mode at its limiting conditions as it does in the intermediate or normal range?) Are there historical examples?

Question: What happens to the adjusting function of the marketplace when the commodity that is scarce is essential to life, such as food or water or oxygen?   Doesn't the "adjusting" take on non-market and non-economic modes such as people dying? Is sole reliance upon the market mechanism (rather than rationing) in a situation of dire scarcity a form of triage done to the poor?

Question: What really is "scarce"? Do economists use this word in one way and other people use it in quite another way? Are economists talking about "relative scarcity" while others mean "absolute scarcity"?

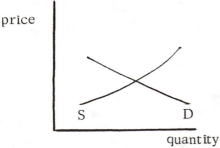

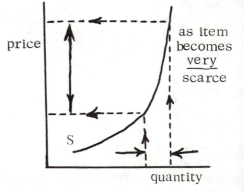

as item becomes <u>very</u> scarce

What You See In Textbooks

The "Limits" Situation of Great Scarcity that Textbooks Don't Consider

Limits to the Market-and-Price Mechanism

At the limits
(as the quantity of an item becomes
very small)

--<u>price increases do not increase supply</u>
    if there simply is no more
(they only decrease demand by consumers)

--price increases cause supply of essential
    items to be <u>used up faster.</u>

i.e. TILT against future generations

--price increases <u>drive the poor</u>
    (not necessarily the less needy)
    <u>out of the market.</u>

Dunagin's People by Ralph Dunagin.
Courtesy of Field Newspaper Syndicate.

i.e. TILT against the poor
and toward the rich.

5.
The Profitability Limits of the Marketplace as an Adjustment Mechanism

The way the marketplace tends to adjust imbalances of supply
and demand is by price increases that motivate profit-maximizing
suppliers. (See "Limitations of the Marketplace," in "Readings.")

<u>Question</u>: Under what conditions -- apart from the limiting condition
    discussed above -- will a price increase <u>not</u> increase supply?

<u>Question</u>: What will be the effect upon the supply and cost of labor
    of the increased emphasis upon finding and extracting materials?
    Will labor productivity pose a profitability constraint upon supply?

<u>Question</u>: What will be the capital costs of new investment to find
    and extract the needed supply? Will we want to afford these
    prices in the goods that result, when we consider the total
    cost of projected energy and material needs as a total percentage
    cost of GNP?

<u>Question</u>: What will be the net-energy profitability? (See Howard T.
    Odum, "Energy, Ecology, and Economics" in the "Readings" on
    "Resource Availability.") Is there not a point of diminishing returns
    from the energy put in compared with the increase in supply that
    is achieved? Do we have any idea where this limit is?

Question: Is the market-and-price mechanism rigged to mask energy-based accounting costs? Is what we see as dollar-inflation that mask? (See "Cosmic Energetics," prepared by The Center for Applied Energetics, Office of the Governor, State of Oregon. See "Readings" on "Adjustment Mechanisms.")

Question: What is the relation of "dollar inflation of prices" to the net energy concept, and to its corollary of diminishing returns in net energy?

Diminishing returns

Editorial cartoon by John Fischetti.
Courtesy of Field Newspaper Syndicate

Question: Are not profitability limits another sort of "limiting condition" for the adjustment capabilities of the market-and-price mechanisms?

6.
Monopoly and Oligopoly Limits of Marketplace Adjustment to Scarcity

The Organization of Petroleum Exporting Countries (OPEC)
has given us a vivid lesson in how organized profit-seeking cartels
can be a limitation of the free functioning of the market-and-price
mechanism. The cartel, not imbalance between supply and demand,
sets the market price. M. A. Adelman's article "Is There An Oil
Shortage?" (see "Readings") is a classic account of this sort of
limit at work in the marketplace for oil.

Question: Can we expect exporter cartels for other resources?
(See "Readings" on "Resource Availability," especially
"One, Two, Many OPEC's . . . ?")

Question: What are the political and economic ramifications
of increased reliance upon oil and other resources from
foreign sources?

Question: What are the economic, social, and political costs of
self-sufficiency in energy and resources? (See "Readings"
on "Resource Availability," especially the Wall Street Journal
series on the costs of energy independence.)

Question: The Ford Foundation's Energy Policy Project recommends
government policies to eliminate institutional obstacles so that
the marketplace can function more effectively. (Exploring Energy
Choices, A Preliminary Report of the Ford Foundation's Energy
Policy Project, p. 47) What policies should be changed? What
would be the effect of such changes?

7.
The Stability of Value of Financial Assets as a Marketplace Limit

The marketplace as an exchange mechanism involves not only
goods but money. The value or price of the goods is assumed to be
variable but the value of the money is assumed to be fixed. So
long as suppliers of goods prefer to hold money rather than goods,
the marketplace can function to bring supply and demand into balance.
But if suppliers should decide that it is going to be more profitable
(or less risky) to hang onto their goods and avoid financial assets,
then the market-and-price mechanism reaches still another limit.
(See "Limitations of the Marketplace" in the "Readings.")

"THE HECK WITH THE MONEY—LET'S PUT THE FOOD IN THE SAFE."

Inflation, currency devaluation, currency inconvertibility into other currencies or into gold, the threat of financial assets being expropriated, "frozen," or otherwise seized -- all these make money and financial assets more risky and comparatively less attractive relative to real goods than when the value of financial assets is fixed and sure.   When the value of financial assets as well as the value (price) of goods changes, suppliers will maximize profits by holding whichever assets do this best.

8.
Government Policy and the Marketplace

The government has long-since accepted the necessity of the marketplace and the necessity of regulating the marketplace in order that the market-and-price mechanism may function efficiently.

Question: What can (or should) the government do to protect the economy and the people from rapid changes in prices?

Question: Is the government's interest in the functioning of the other markets comparable to its interest in the functioning of the capital markets? If so, is there need for further non-private, non-governmental "trustee" charters comparable to that of the Federal Reserve System's charter?

Many government policies are not directed at the marketplace but affect how the marketplace functions. For example, government support of the mortgage market for single-family dwellings following World War II had the effect of encouraging an energy-demanding housing and transportation system in the suburbs.

Question: How can government policy be changed to encourage market decisions in favor of conservation (efficiency in use and hence reduced demand) rather than consumption of energy and resources? (See Ford Foundation Energy Policy Project preliminary report, pp. 47f. in "Readings" on "Energy: A Case Study.")

Where market solutions are not feasible, direct regulation may be required. (See the Introduction and Readings of the sections on "Resource Availability" and "Environmental Pollution" for elaboration.)

Question: Have we identified the conditions under which market solutions are not feasible?

SELECTED READINGS

Adelman, M. A., "Is the Oil Shortage Real?" Foreign Policy, Winter 1972.

Bell, Daniel, "The Subordination of the Corporation: The Tension between the Economizing and Sociologizing Modes," in The Coming of Post-Industrial Society: A Venture in Social Forecasting. New York: Basic Books, 1973.

Gray, David Dodson, "Limitations of the Marketplace" in Growth and Its Implications for the Future, Vol. 3. Washington: Government Printing Office, 1974.

Henderson, Hazel, "Taking the Measure of John Kenneth Galbraith: A Review of Economics and the Public Purpose" in Business and Society, December 11, 1973.

7

TECHNOLOGY AS AN ADJUSTMENT MECHANISM

SUMMARY

1. Basic Issues

2. The Current Debate

3. Technology Assessment

   3.1 From Reductionist Thinking to Holistic Thinking
   3.2 Technology Assessment as "Seeing the Widening Circle of Effects"
   3.3 Technology Assessment as "Input/Output" Analysis

4. Technology as an Adjustment Mechanism

   4.1 Technology and the Development of Energy Sources
   4.2 Technology and the Availability of Material Resources
   4.3 Technology and Environmental Effects
   4.4 Technology and Population, Food and Land Use
   4.5 Technology and People
   4.6 New Priorities for Technology

1.
Basic Issues

Question: Can technology provide solutions to the basic problems
resulting from economic growth and population increases?
How likely are technological advances to help population and
food problems? Resource availability? Energy sources?
Environmental degradation?

Question: How can we protect ourselves from unanticipated side
effects of technological solutions?

Question: What sorts of social change and rates of social change
are implied by specific technological solutions?

2.
The Current Debate

We are ambivalent about technology. Technology is viewed both
as potential savior and as destructive monster. Some aspects of
technology have served us well in the past, but we must ask if it must
not play a rather different role in the future.

There is a growing uneasiness with the "technology evermore"
ethic. The 1971 rejection of the SST project by the United States
Congress illustrates the extent to which there is a dawning awareness
that technology may on occasion have dangerous environmental effects.
Others see a potential invasion of individual privacy. Still others are
concerned about the scale of social organization involved, the complexity
of many solutions, and the assumptions sometimes being made about
risks and the likelihood of accidents as well as about the reliability of
human nature and institutions.

Question: Are we able to master and control our own technology?

Technology has been compared to a medicine, used to relieve
unpleasant symptoms while leaving untreated the underlying social
ills. From this perspective technology is seen as sometimes inducing
a dependence effect and as potentially addictive. (See "Long-Term
Constraints on Human Activity," by Amory Lovins. "Readings.")

Question: Is technology inherently addictive, forcing society into
further crises demanding further technological fixes until the
habit becomes socially unsustainable?

113

Harvey Brooks of Harvard, writing about "The Technology of Zero Growth," maintains that a sophisticated technology will be necessary even in a no-growth society and that "we cannot simply retrac our past industrial and technological progress back to some simpler society." (Daedalus, Fall 1973, p. 152. "Readings.")

Among those who view technology as potential savior, technology is seen as a major adjustment mechanism that we have used in the past and will continue to use in the future in coping with problems. When resource scarcity causes prices to rise (the market-and-price mechanism), then technology will be pushed to utilize heretofore uneconomic means for resource extraction from lower-grade reserves, for increasing food supplies, and for eliminating accompanying environmental pollution through more sophisticated pollution abatement equipment. As J. K. Galbraith once put it, "It is a commonplace of modern technology that problems have solutions before there is knowledge of how they are to be solved." (For an example of this view see "Resource Shortages in an Expanding World," by Wilfred Malenbaum. Wharton Quarterly, Winter 1973. "Readings" on "Resource Availability.")

Question: Are there environmental effects which known and imagined technologies cannot solve?

3.
Technology Assessment

3.1
From Reductionist Thinking to Holistic Thinking

The manner in which our forefathers challenged earlier frontiers represents a practical application of a simple, yet effective, technology. The commons in the West was large and the scale of their technology was modest. One man's technology didn't cramp another's living space. Today's technology functions within a socio-economic system on an entirely different scale, and in a system in which technology has become much more complicated and dominant. It occupies a much larger place in all our lives and we are much more dependent upon it. What biologists have known for a long time about organic systems -- that "you can never do just one thing" (Garrett Hardin) -- we are now beginning to see is also true of the complex interactions of social systems. We live in a system which is so interdependent that everything interacts in ways we are just beginning to comprehend. (See Hardin's "What the Hedgehog Knows" in "Readings.")

The need, then, is to think "holistically," to consider not just the pebble that drops into the pond but the widening circle of ripples as well.

Technology, however, has characteristically moved not holistically but linearly -- from cause to effect, from problem to solution -- in an intense and narrowly focused way that traditionally has not been concerned with side effects of its solutions. "The fault," Barry Commoner has written, "is reductionism, the view that effective understanding of a complex system can be achieved by investigating the properties of its isolated parts." (The Closing Circle, p. 187)

Commoner is a trenchant critic of technology as it is presently used and of the "ecological surprises" it too frequently springs upon us. However he asserts that "technology properly guided by appropriate scientific knowledge can be successful in the ecosystem, if its aims are directed toward the system as a whole rather than at some apparently accessible part. . . . Ecological survival does not mean the abandonment of technology. Rather, it requires that technology be derived from a scientific analysis that is appropriate to the natural world on which technology intrudes." (p. 186f. Italics added.)

3.2
Technology Assessment as "Seeing the Widening Circle of Effects"

We spoke earlier of the need to consider "not just the pebble that drops into the pond but the widening circle of ripples as well." Technology as employed in the past has always produced a series of first, second, and other effects. We have often called these later effects "side effects" but they are all equally direct effects of technology. It is just that they were not the effects intended or anticipated from the technology.

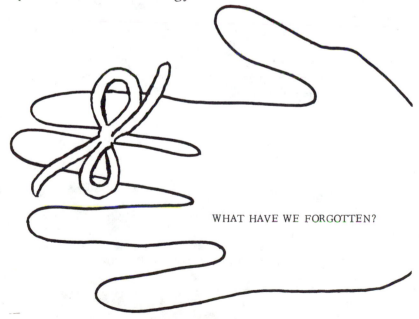

WHAT HAVE WE FORGOTTEN?

We can categorize the "levels" at which these effects occur as follows:

I. The immediate solution or benefit to which the technology was primarily addressed.

II. The environmental changes caused by the technology. Only recently have we begun to perceive that the resource depletion and the byproduct wastes of a technology are as much a direct outcome of a technology as all the first-level "intended" or "desired" effects.

III. The social changes that accompany an innovation, or that an innovation made possible and thus followed from the technology, are a third level of direct effects of a technology. The social order made possible and implied by a technology also is a product of that technology. Here we think of the effects of technology upon the scale of institutions and communities. We look for the diversity or homogeneity of a culture and its subcultures that new practices may encourage or erode. We look for changes in patterns of interdependence or independence as it affects individuals, communities and regions. We look at the flexibility and stability of a culture and economy, and their ability to adapt to a range of input availabilities and output demands. (Comparable environmental changes in diversity, stability and resiliancy must also be considered in Level II.)

IV. Society's use of technology as a palliative rather than a problem-solver, as a pain-killer and mask for social problems, is a fourth level of direct effect. A tech-fix that treats symptoms may not (but often does) help society avoid addressing itself to the more fundamental task of finding social means to "heal" social problems. This effect of technology is addictive, and it induces a societal orientation that becomes physically and biologically as well as psychologically, culturally, institutionally, and politically "dependent" upon ever more tech "fixes" to avoid facing its mounting ills that continue to pile up unresolved and unaddressed.

V. Catalytic effects upon other systems. The different "level-effects" listed above interact producing results that defy the adage that "the whole equals the sum of all its parts." In practice many of the palliative, social and environmental effects exacerbate the overall impact of each. These "fifth-level" effects are observed most vividly in the limiting situations, when the original expanding circles of ripple effects are reflected back into the fourth and third and second and first-level effects. The spreading system of technological effects is then getting feedback effects from other systems. Then we see that the most fundamental and basic product of technology is not the immediate product or particular benefit nor any of the other earlier level effects. The most far-reaching and ultimately significant effect of technology is its tremendous leverage upon the overall condition and vitality of all our essential life-support systems of the biosphere (nature) and ethosphere (society).

The major product, then, of technology is its catalytic effect upon our system-settings -- our setting within the system of persons aware of living in history and society as well as our setting within an impersonal setting we call the natural environment.

Assessment of an innovation's impact must be directed at the whole system, rather than just at some apparently more accessible part. Costs as well as benefits have to be weighed in more than dollar terms, more than just in environmental terms -- so that societal costs and benefits, addictive costs and benefits, and catalytic system-wide effects are questioned.

Let us now consider some important technology-assessment questions, keeping in mind the several levels of direct effect which may be involved. An interesting example of this sort of assessment, though "after the fact," is Lester R. Brown's assessment of the impact of the Green Revolution technology upon developing countries. (See "Population and Affluence," pp. 10-11 in "Readings" for the section on "Population, Food and Land.")

Question: What is the energy input and material-resource input of this new technology? If the new technology will have an energy output or resource output, what is the net energy budget? (See Odum, et al., on energetics and net energy -- "Readings" in the "Resource Availability" section.)

Question: What is the social-change input that will have to accompany the new technology? The political-change input?

Question: How complex (or simple) is the new technology?

The degree of complexity is a measure of possible complication and probable delay in developing and implementing a technology. A complex technology is seldom a quick tech-fix. For example, natural gas involved a simple technology and went in about twenty-five years from providing approximately 10% of the U.S. energy input to more than 30%; in those same years after World War II nuclear fission was known to be a possible source of commercial energy but only in the twenty-fifth year did nuclear energy (with its more complex technology) provide more energy to the U.S. than firewood did -- 1%.

Question: How subject is the new technology to breakdown? (Again the complexity question.) How subject to technical or human error? To sabotage? To unintended conversion to military or political uses hostile to the United States?

Question: How will the new technology affect other systems? Economic? Monetary? Balance of payments? International political? Internal political or social systems of other countries? Technical systems? Environmental systems?

Question: Is the new technology addictive? (Does it generate its own need for more?) Does the new technology relieve the pain of symptoms, or does it get at underlying social problems and pathologies?

3.3
Technology Assessment as "Input/Output" Analysis

Another mental framework within which it is useful to assess technology involves systematic input/output analysis of the complex multi-level system of effects outlined above. The diagram below suggests the rudiments of such an analysis. One way or another, these sorts of complex cost-and-benefit analyses are a necessary step toward a safe and livable future.

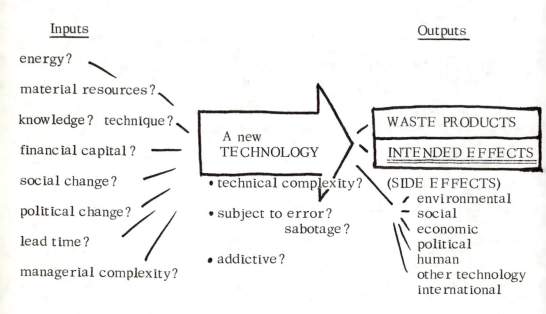

The Input/Output Model of Technology Assessment

4.
Technology as an Adjustment Mechanism

4.1
Technology and the Development of Energy Sources

The following are current or projected energy sources or technologies:

--Fossil fuels: coal, petroleum, natural gas
--Coal gasification and liquification
--Solar power
--Nuclear power (fission, fusion)
--Shale oil
--Tar sands
--Wind power
--Tidal and hydroelectric power
--Geothermal power
--Biogas (energy generation from solid wastes)
--Magnetohydrodynamics (converting thermal energy
    directly to electrical energy without the intermediate
    step of mechanical work)

Question: What is the net energy prospect for each source? (How
    much of the energy that is produced has to go back into producing
    the next unit of energy?

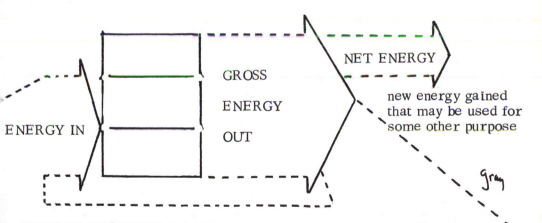

ENERGY IN

GROSS

ENERGY

OUT

NET ENERGY

new energy gained
that may be used for
some other purpose

gray

ENERGY REQUIRED TO DEVELOP AND RUN THE PROCESS

(to develop the technology to do it
(to train researchers to develop the technology
(to sustain the researchers from birth through training to development
    and the energy after development
(to produce the machinery, deliver it to the site, and
(after it is extracted, to get the energy to markets where it will be used.

Question: What is the quality (versatility) of the energy produced? (Solar energy for space-heating purposes is comparatively simple; solar energy to power an automobile or run an electric motor is a different matter.)

Question: What substitutions among energy sources are possible, so that low-grade energy is used wherever possible and high-grade energy used where only it will do? (For example, we can use solar energy for space heating homes in order to conserve the more versatile fossil fuels for other uses.)

Question: Is the needed technology complex or simple? Is it at hand, known to be possible, or only theoretically possible?

Question: Can the technology be used to reduce energy demand? To increase efficiency in the use of energy? To diminish the loss of energy? (For example, better insulation.) To transform "thermal pollution" from an effluent problem into a source of "low-grade" heat?

4.2
Technology and the Availability of Material Resources

Problems with the availability of material resources suggest that we seek new technologies that might help us in the following areas:

- --the search for additional supplies
- --the discovery of synthetic substitutes for critical exhausted minerals
- --recycling technology
- --mining increasingly lower grade reserves in increasingly remote and inaccessible areas
- --mining the ocean floor

We must inquire of possible new technologies about the following possible constraints:

- --energy costs?
- --financial costs?
- --environmental costs?

- --fresh water needs?
- --social change inputs?
- --social sacrifices/tradeoffs?

4.3
Technology and Environmental Effects

The environmental effects to which technology contributes and with which we should seek technology's help are suggested by the following:

--mercury and other toxic heavy metals
--DDT and related persistent pesticides
--waste treatment and excess nutrients in inland or coastal waters
--ecological and land disruption caused by the extraction of materials
--oil spills, both chronic low-level and catastrophic
--neutralizing or sufficiently securing the long-term storage
  of radioactive nuclear wastes
--assuring that nuclear fission materials are safe from theft
  or sabotage
--eliminating, reducing, or neutralizing toxic effects of pollutants
  upon agricultural and industrial workers
--monitoring, assessing, and limiting the buildup of carbon
  dioxide and other materials (particles, gases) released
  into the atmosphere
--monitoring, assessing, and taking early action in high-risk
  situations (e.g. polyvinyl chloride, asbestos)
--environmental assessment of the routes of distribution
  of pollutants, their eventual distribution in the environment,
  and their passage through ecosystems
--effects upon climate and changes in world-wide heat-flows
  and thermal-energy balance

4.4
Technology and Population, Food and Land Use

According to Lester R. Brown:

Following the discovery of agriculture 10,000 or more years
ago, food production expanded under the influence of six major
technological advances:
    --the use of irrigation
    --the harnessing of draft animals
    --the exchange of crops between the Old World and the New
    --the development of chemical fertilizers and pesticides
    --the invention of the internal combustion engine.

Technological advances in agriculture and consequent increases
in food supply have permitted population to increase. Population
increases in turn generate pressures for agricultural innovation.
Thus trends of expanding food production and growing population
have reinforced each other.

There are essentially two ways of expanding food supply
from conventional agriculture. One is to expand the area
under cultivation. The other, largely made possible by the
advancements in the use of agricultural chemicals and in plant
genetics, is to raise output on the existing cultivated area.

At the global level, the record of the past two decades suggests it is far cheaper and easier to expand the food supply by intensifying cultivation on the existing cropland area than by bringing new land under the plow.

In assessing the results of this Green Revolution, Dr. Brown notes

. . . It was a means of buying time, perhaps an additional 15 or 20 years during which the brakes could be applied to population growth. Ultimately the only solution to the food problem will be the curbing of world population growth.

(See "Population and Affluence: Growing Pressures on World Food Resources," by Lester R. Brown, pp. 4, 6, 8, 10. Population Bulletin 29:2 from Population Reference Bureau, Inc. See "Readings" in the section "Population, Food and Land.")

Question: What effect will a given new technology have upon the complex system of population, food and land use?

Question: Will a given new technology compete with the population, food and land-use system for inputs? What will be the effects of that competition upon price, demand and supply of those inputs? (Land, water, energy, capital, labor, skills, production-oriented incentives)

Question: Will a given new technology affect, directly or indirectly, the outputs of the population, food and land-use system? In quantity? Quality? Trend?

Question: What is the likelihood of new technologies that could alleviate undesirable side-effects of one of the six major technological advances Lester Brown cites?

Question: What is the likelihood of new technologies increasing the per/acre yield of soybeans? (This single breakthrough would be most helpful in increasing the world protein supply.)

Question: What is the likelihood of technologies shifting consumer food habits from animal proteins toward vegetable proteins? (It takes seven to ten cereal calories to produce one calorie "on the hoof," so animal calories are the end-product of a wasteful (or expensive) calorie-conversion process.)

4.5
Technology and People

Question: What is the effect of technology upon the rate of change
    that people experience in their life-settings? Upon the
    complexity of that change?

Question: What is the effect of technology upon the interior life
    of individuals (upon motivation, loyalty patterns, courage,
    sense of meaning, sense of potency or impotence regarding
    life's direction and significance, sense of life's "making sense"
    and being "comprehendible")?

Question: What is the effect of technology upon individuals'
    interdependence upon one another? Upon their independence
    of one another?

Question: What is the effect of technology upon our independence
    of the total social system? Upon our interdependence upon
    one another and the system?

The One Who Has the Impact

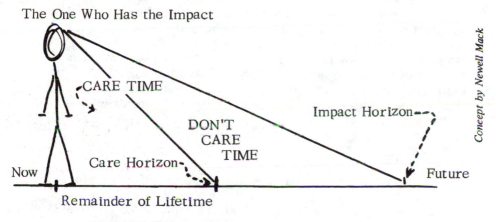

Care Horizon vs. Impact Horizon for Any Action

Question: Who then will an innovation benefit? Who will pay the
    cost? Are they the same? (The following question expands upon this.)

Question: What is the impact horizon of an innovation? In space?
    In time? Does the impact horizon exceed our "care" horizon in
    either space or time? How sizable is the "don't-care" time
    beyond our care time and the innovation's impact time-horizon?

Question: What are the social power changes implied by a certain
    technology? Does it change who gets to decide something?
    Does it change how many people get things decided for them?
    Who gets more power and who gets less? Is the authority or power
    part of a zero-sum game, or of a positive-sum game?

Question: What effect has technology had upon the meaning of
work and perceived social roles for men? For women? For
children? For different economic and social classes?

Question: What effect has technology had upon the nature of our
social institutions and the personal qualities (character,
personality, talents, skills) that these institutions evoke,
reward, and project into top leadership roles?

Question: Does technology, functioning as one of the prime catalysts
within the whole life-system, affect some parts of the life-system
scarcely at all and others a great deal?

4.6
New Priorities for Technology

"The better mouse trap" was a technology designed to bring
people to your door so you could make a profitable living. It wasn't
simply a device to bring you people who had a problem you could
solve, or to bring you a crowd just for crowding's sake. Profit
has been a very powerful incentive that has sped the introduction
of much of our technology. Technology has developed products
and processes that met specific needs and that could be sold at a
profit. Technology has suggested efficiencies, substitutions, or
improvements that lowered costs, often thus decreasing prices
and so increasing demand. In all this technology has often been
a servant of profit.

But profit is not the only possible motive for developing and
introducing technologies. Getting to the moon (NASA) and
better medical practice (NIH) had other primary motivations than
profit. We need to consider briefly other motivations for the
introduction of technology -- motivations which may be more life-
system sensitive and less life-system disruptive than the profit-
driven technologies of the past frequently have been.

Question: How can technology be motivated to switch from a
throw-away orientation to the reuse, repair, recycle of the
Ford Foundation's Energy Policy Project third scenario?

Question: How do we switch from profit-maximizing technologies
to technologies that emphasize product durability and energy
efficiency? Can the market-and-price mechanism and its
profit incentives do this?

Question: How can the time parameters of technological solutions
be shifted from an emphasis upon short "useful product lifetimes"
(followed often by long "wastetimes") to an emphasis upon much
longer useful product lifetimes (followed by short, biodegradable
wastetimes)? (We need longer useful lifetimes and short
biodegradable wastetimes for products, if we are to minimize
material-resource inputs and maximize recovery and reuse
of wastes.)

Question: How can the scale of technological solutions be shifted away
from an emphasis upon bigness and complexity and toward what
E. F. Schumacher calls "intermediate technology," which is
more suitable to many needs and locations in both developed and
developing countries? (See E. F. Schumacher, Small Is Beautiful
in "Readings.")

Question: What are the necessary social mechanisms for shifting
technology from its use as an instrument of profit to use as
an instrument for achieving social goals?

SELECTED READINGS

Bell, Daniel, "Varieties of Planning," in The Coming of Post-
Industrial Society: A Venture in Social Forecasting. New York:
Basic Books, 1973.

Brooks, Harvey, "The Technology of Zero Growth" in Daedalus,
Fall 1973.

Commoner, Barry, "The Social Issues" in The Closing Circle: Nature
Man and Technology. New York: Alfred Knopf, Inc., 1971.

Galbraith, John Kenneth, "The Revised Economics of Technical
Innovation" in Economics and the Public Purpose. Boston:
Houghton Mifflin Co., 1973.

Hardin, Garrett, "What the Hedgehog Knows" in Exploring New Ethics
for Survival. New York: Viking, 1972.

Kahn, Herman and B. Bruce-Briggs, "The 1985 Technological Crisis --
The Social Effects of Technology" in Things to Come: Thinking
about the Seventies and Eighties. New York: Macmillan Co., 1972.

Ophuls, William, "Technological Limits to Growth Revisited" in
Growth and Its Implications for the Future, Vol. 3. Washington:
Government Printing Office, 1974.

Schumacher, E. F., Small Is Beautiful. New York: Harper and Row,
1973.

8

CONSCIOUSNESS: THE TUNNEL FROM HERE TO THERE

Woven like a golden strand

through all of the Gordian knots we have wrestled to untie

is that subtle, elusive factor of "consciousness."

About population control, an official says forebodingly,

"You are trying to reshape the thinking of mankind."*

About limiting growth, the Rockefeller Land-Use Study proclaims

a significant shift in attitudes about growth in local communities.**

The Ford Foundation study of energy futures talks of

possible changes in life-style.

The environmentalists talk of "quality of life,"

and Limits to Growth itself, in its conclusion, speakings movingly about

"The final, most elusive, and most important information we need

deals with human values."***

Values, attitudes, expectations, hopes, fears, roles --

all are a part of that intangible, unquantifiable,

yet terribly real way in which we see ourselves, our society, our world.

This is what we shall call "consciousness."

* In "World Population: U.N. on the Move but Grounds for Optimism are Scant,"
by Constance Holden. *Science,* March 1974.

** *The Use of Land,* A Task Force Report Sponsored by the Rockefeller
Brothers Fund, p. 33.

*** *Limits,* p. 181

CONSCIOUSNESS: THE TUNNEL FROM HERE TO THERE

SUMMARY

1. The Attitudes of People Permeate Every Problem

2. Responses to Consciousness

3. Consciousness Is in Flux

4. Consciousness in America: Where We have Come From

5. Consciousness in America: Where Are We Now?

6. Consciousness in America: Where Do We Go From Here?

7. Our Widening Field of Vision

8. Can We Think "Whole" or Only in Parts?

9. Adjusting to Limits

10. Redoing Our Sense of Our Relationship with Nature

1.
The Attitudes of People Permeate Every Problem

As we wrestle to understand the parameters of growth and its implications for the future, we find that each area to which we turn seems to have its own quota of "intangibles."

--The decision to have (or not to have) more children emerges from a mixture of luck, planning, social, religious and personal feelings, and circumstance.

--A complex mixture of national needs, team spirit, and corporate goals push competing fishing fleets to overfish the oceans.

--The drive to hold or expand markets and to maximize profit and personal careers leads industry to continue polluting despite hazards to health and ecosystems.

--Two sets of scientists have the same data about the availability of natural resources; one group gives out ominous warnings while the other is confident new discoveries (or new technologies, or the effective working of the marketplace) are right around the corner.

YOU
THINK
FUNNY

Courtesy of Argus Communications

--Environmental "costs" of the operation of our economic system are just becoming visible, partly because of a "tilt" in our consciousness so that only dollars and "quantifiables" are real enough to factor into business decisions: efforts to "put a dollar-value on saving the Grand Canyon" and class assignments to "quantify a smile" are evidences of this tilt.

--Some suggest that our technological advances are addictive, each "tech fix" requiring still another.

--Population experts debate whether lower birth rates result from the availability of birth control programs or from rising affluence.

--World food experts bemoan the new "taste" for animal protein in countries with rising affluence.

<u>Question:</u> We are confronted by attitudes and thought-worlds and frames of reference at every turn. Can these "intangibles" be understood? Can they be changed? If so, how?

2.
Responses to Consciousness

One response to all this "soft" data is to retreat back to the world of numbers, machines, rational science, bottom-line profit making, and "hard" data. Consciousness seems too elusive even to work with. But though it may seem too elusive, it is also pervasive. "Soft data" is what was left out of decisions based upon "hard data"-- decisions that too frequently bungle the original intentions of the decision-makers.

Values, roles, expectations about life and about life-styles, are difficult to get at. But as M.I.T.'s Jay W. Forrester has observed, we have already found the technological solutions to the easy problems, and now we are coming up against the hard problems that don't yield easily to technical solutions because they involve social problems and social systems. Our intangibles are also "reals."

Grin and Bear It by George Lichty. Courtesy of Field Newspaper Syndicate.

"As a liberated female I'm not going to be anybody's valentine until I've read the contract and job description!"

Another retreat from dealing with consciousness involves people deciding that the roots of our thought worlds are so deeply embedded in people's psyches that they seem immutable. Such is the lament about population control: "You are trying to reshape the thinking of mankind." Such is the conviction of those who hold that social roles of men and women are rooted in our pre-history as hunters and gatherers, and thus are too deeply rooted and basic ever to change significantly.

As David Dodson Gray has pointed out in "The Human Dimensions of Limiting Growth" (see "Readings"), our attitudes toward growth do have deep psychic roots. "In addition to being an economic and physical fact, growth has become a powerful internalized symbol with vast psychic ramifications." Growth has been our economic goal, our personal goal, our social goal. "Things are new, or more, or better, seldom old, or less, or not the biggest." (pp. 1, 3)

Question: Is such a massive social goal susceptible to change? To modification or replacement?

Question: What might have the power and attractiveness as a social goal to replace it?

Question: Can a whole society change such a major portion of what it feels its life and its institutions and its success are all about?

Adapted from *Yale Alumni Magazine*

Despite the deep psychic rootage of many of our attitudes and values, the Rockefeller Land-Use study points to a re-evaluation of our attitudes toward the idea of growth, at least growth as it is perceived by local communities:

Once, citizens automatically accepted the idea that growth -- in numbers of people, in jobs, in taxes, in industries -- would ease the public burden by increasing the tax rolls and spreading per capita costs. Now they have doubts. They seem to be expressing the belief that large size means not only lesser quality but also higher costs. Pressed by inflation, they listen carefully to arguments about the hidden costs of growth.

The new mood reflects a burgeoning sophistication on the part of citizens about the overall, long-term economic impact of development. Immediate economic gains from job creation, land purchases, and the construction of new facilities are being set against the public costs of schools, roads, water-treatment plants, sewers, and the services new residents require.

But the new attitude toward growth is not exclusively motivated by economics. It appears to be part of a rising emphasis on humanism, on the preservation of natural and cultural character- istics that make for a humanly satisfying living environment. (pp. 33-34)

Question: Have we already begun as a people re-evaluating our older pro-growth orientation?

3.
Consciousness Is in Flux

Often we do not perceive the slow changes in consciousness that take place around us. But as former Senator Ernest Gruening observed,

The taboo of the day before yesterday becomes the controversial of yesterday, the accepted of today, and the wanted of tomorrow.*

Garrett Hardin is interesting in his observations about the rate at which consciousness sometimes changes.

History has . . . given a critical testing of the conventional wisdom that it takes generations to bring about change in highly emotional areas. Few areas were as emotional as abortion in

* Cited in Holden, "U.N. on the Move." (See "Readings" of the section on "Population, Food and Land Use.")

1963, yet it took only ten years, not a hundred, for a small band of abortion activists to create a new climate of opinion on which the Supreme Court Decision (January 1973) could rest.*

The Rockefeller Land-Use study has a large opening section on "Challenging the Ideal of Growth: A New Mood in America."

There have been isolated instances of such reactions before, of course. But today, the repeated questioning of what was once generally unquestioned -- that growth is good, that growth is inevitable -- is so widespread that it seems to us to signal a remarkable change in attitudes in this nation. (p. 33. Italics added.)

It is this "repeated questioning of what was once generally unquestioned" that constitutes a fascinating change of consciousness about growth. That change of consciousness -- what has already taken place and that which may or should take place in the future -- is a vital, if intangible, link in our chain of thinking about "Growth and Its Implications for the Future" and consciousness as a tunnel by which our minds get from here to that future.

Question: Would you agree with the Rockefeller Land-Use report that growth is being questioned in our society?

4.
Consciousness in America: Where We Have Come From

The American consciousness has undergone significant shifts through the years. As David and Elizabeth Dodson Gray point out in their paper "Harnessing Our Will to Survive" (see "Readings"), "this country was founded by plain-dressing, plain-living Puritans," but when our "manufacturing capacity . . . could produce more than a nation of frugal drudges wanted to consume," we changed, under the sweet goad of advertising, to a consciousness now rich in materialism, consumerism, "buy now and pay later." A similar shift occurred, the Grays point out, from the rugged individualism of the frontier to the great conformity that provides the work force necessary for our mass-production economy -- even while our ideology of "individualism" continues to function like a myth in our midst.

---

* "Changing Attitudes of Society" in *Alternative Futures and Environmental Quality*, a publication of the Environmental Protection Agency, 1973.

The historian Frederick Jackson Turner wrote about the influence of the frontier experience upon the American character.* David Potter, in his more recent book <u>People of Plenty</u>, has done an interesting study of the effect of abundance on the American character.

> America has long been famous as a land of plenty, but we seldom realize how much the American people are a "people of plenty" -- a people whose distinctive character has been shaped by economic abundance.**

Adapted from *The Institutional Investor*

* Frederick Jackson Turner, "The Significance of the Frontier in American History" (1893) in *The Frontier in American History* (New York: Henry Holt and Co., 1920).

** David M. Potter, *People of Plenty: Economic Abundance and the American Character* (Chicago: University of Chicago Press, 1954). The quotation is from the back cover of the paperback edition.

Question: Are Americans now "addicted" to abundance?

Question: Are we capable of going back (or forward) to a simple life again?

Question: Are there motifs in our "attic" (as the Grays suggest) that would make a simpler life seem "native American"?

5.
Consciousness in America: Where Are We Now?

George Cabot Lodge of the Harvard Business School has pointed out that the major elements of our traditional American ideology are rooted in the thought of John Locke and can be summarized as "individualism, property rights, competition, the limited state, and Newtonian science with its companion notion of specialization."* A very similar summary of American ideology is found in the study of Changing Images of Man done by the Center for the Study of Social Policy at the Stanford Research Institute. Changing Images of Man characterizes what it calls the Economic Image of Man as "rationalistic, mechanistic, individualistic, and materialistic." (p. 54. See "Readings.")

Both George Cabot Lodge and Changing Images of Man suggest that this traditional American ideology is being eroded under the pressure of contemporary problems and malaise. Lodge writes that:

> The great individualistic, proprietary, competitive thrust with its enormous technological and economic achievements is faltering; the Lockean blip is ending. We are seeking new social and political constructions which will clearly embrace economic and technological activity and allow for the development of a new sense of community; the atomistic is giving way to the organic, the parts to the whole, the linear to the circular, the sensate to the ideational." (Lodge, p. 2)

Changing Images of Man sees the transition in evolutionary terms:

> Such premises were very appropriate for the transition from a world made up of low-technology agrarian endeavors and city-states to one dominated by high-technology nation-states; they helped provide a seemingly ideal way to increase man's standard of living and to bring problems of physical survival under control.

---

* George Cabot Lodge, *The New American Ideology* (forthcoming).

. . . But their successful realization has resulted in an interconnected set of urgent societal problems which likely cannot
be resolved through continued use of those premises; they now
appear ill-suited for the further transition to a planetary society
that would distribute its affluence equitably, regulate itself
humanely, and embody appropriate images of the further future.
(Changing Images of Man, p. vi)

It is important to note that, while Lodge and Changing Images of
Man disagree about what is emerging, they are in total agreement
that the traditional ideology is disintegrating.

Daniel Bell, writing in his latest book, The Coming of Post-
Industrial Society, sees the end of the classic economic liberalism
of John Locke and Adam Smith in which we relied upon "the invisible
hand" to transmute our individual choices into a common good.
Like Lodge, Bell sees us moving from an individualistic ethic to
a communal ethic that will be expressed in the conscious choice of
goals and priorties through our political decisions, not through the
working of the marketplace.   Such a development Bell sees as
inevitable because individualistic decisions have impacted unfavorably
upon the public good.   He sees the shift to anticipating consequences
and making conscious choices a necessary shift, far preferable to
cleaning up afterwards when there are unanticipated problems.

Question: Do you see evidence that such a dominant image of man
         is breaking up in our culture?

Question: What do you see emerging as the dominant image of
         humankind that may take its place?

6.
Consciousness in America: Where Do We Go From Here?

Changing Images of Man foresees and hopes for what it calls
an "evolutionary transformationalist" image -- which would be
experimental, holistic, integrative, with a strong ecological and self-
realizational ethic. (p. vii)   The concern of Changing Images of
Man seems to be to find values that will save us.

The direction suggested by the Rockefeller Land-Use study is
quite different but in its own way radical: we Americans must change
our sense of private property as it relates to land and our use of land.

We think it highly likely that in forthcoming decades Americans
will gradually abandon the traditional assumption that
urbanization rights arise from the land itself.   Development
potential on any land and in any community, results largely
from the actions of society (especially the construction of

public facilities). Other free societies, notably Great Britain, have abandoned the old assumption in their legal systems and now treat development rights as created and allocated to the land by society.

What is needed is a changed attitude toward land, not simply a growing awareness of the importance of stewardship, but a separation of commodity rights in the land from urbanization rights. (p. 143)

A shift of consciousness in a different area, this time population policy, is called for by the President's Commission on Population and the American Future. The Commission calls for a shift from a "pro-natalist" orientation to one of neutrality so that we may stabilize our population.

There is yet another assumed orientation that needs to be examined. In her paper "Masculine Consciousness and the Problem of Limiting Growth" Elizabeth Dodson Gray suggests that unacknowledged masculine values supercharge economic growth in our culture. (See "Readings.")

Question: Do these projections of consciousness for the future
         seem fanciful, or are these some "signs in the times"?

Among those who think systematically about the future there is a debate. On the one hand there are those who can see the future as an essential continuation of present trends.   On the other hand there are those who find the problems of the present sufficiently disturbing that they are convinced that the future needs to be a serious correction, if not a repudiation, of much of the present.

Daniel Bell's The Coming of Post-Industrial Society is an example of the future as a continuation of the present trends. He sees the movement from a manufacturing to a service-based economy; from a society in which power and status are based upon property to one in which knowledge expressed in scientific innovation is the basis for power. The research-based university is seen replacing the corporation as the central organization of the future; the new elite will be scientists, economists, and engineers instead of entrepreneurs and businessmen.

In Bell's future we will attempt to anticipate, plan and choose our future.   Advanced science will use computers to simulate alternative futures for a political system that will take communal action in choosing goals and priorities, rather than leaving so much to individualized action and choices through the marketplace. All of Bell's projections for the future assume our present course in science, technology, and progress will continue. (See "Readings.")

There is another group of thinkers who emerge as critics of where we are today, who look into the future and see disaster -- unless there can be deep modification of our ways of thinking and operating.   Robert Heilbroner in his book <u>The Human Prospect</u> expresses this well:

> . . . I believe the long-term solution requires nothing less than the abandonment of the lethal techniques, the uncongenial ways of life, and the dangerous mentality of industrial civilization itself.

> . . . The societal view of production and consumption must stress parsimonius, not prodigal, attitudes. Resource consuming and heat-generating processes must be regarded as necessary evils, not as social triumphs, to be relegated to as small a portion of economic life as possible. This implies a sweeping reorganization of the mode of production in ways that cannot be foretold, but that would seem to imply the end of the giant factory, the huge office, perhaps of the urban complex. (p. 33f. See "Readings.")

<u>Question:</u> How does this debate help us think about where we are and where we need to go?

<u>Question:</u> How may one's life position in the presently dominant intellectual, scientific or societal group affect one's position in such a debate?

7.
Our Widening Field of Vision

A crucial dimension of consciousness is perception or "seeing." Many of the problems with limits can be accounted for as problems with perception: "If we'd known . . ." What an entire society does not see can become a disaster when there is no one to see and say "Our emperor has no clothes!"

Not too long ago what our culture "saw" and "what mattered" in our decision-making were profit and reason. Of course we saw other things too, but they didn't matter usually. Decision-makers -- from the executive suite to the man in the street -- assumed that choices were rational and that they were made to maximize profits. This was simply how decisions were made.

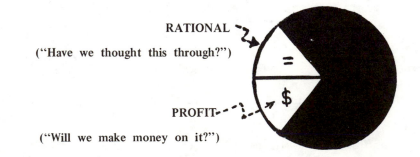

RATIONAL

("Have we thought this through?")

PROFIT

("Will we make money on it?")

Our problems with our environment were always there, but recently they began to mount. Then we realized we hadn't been "seeing" our environment when we made our decisions. The environment hadn't "mattered."

Even more recently we discovered we hadn't been "seeing" energy. We didn't realize we were so energy-dependent and so dependent upon energy being so cheap as well as available. (We still don't make our decisions in terms of "net energy" -- which is like running a business with no sense of net profit.) What we don't see, or don't see the significance of, we don't factor into our decision-making.

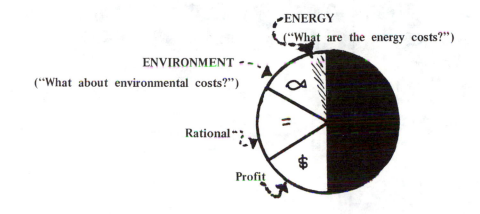

"People" have been affected by rational, profit-oriented decision-making for a long time, but only very recently has it become essential to look at and take account of what is good for

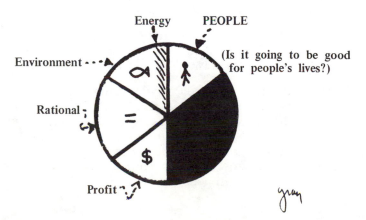

people and people's lives. The phrase "quality of life" suggests the dawning awareness that we may, with the best intentions, construct by our decisions a society that is good for machines and institutions but very hard on people. Work in America, the Report of a Special Task Force to the Secretary of Health, Education, and Welfare, cites as widespread such symptoms of alienation as rising absenteeism, alcoholism, on-the-job use of drugs, poor productivity, problems with motivation and morale, greatly increased employee theft, and sabotage. (MIT Press, 1973. See in "Readings" "The Human Dimensions of Limiting Growth," by David Dodson Gray.)

Next year, will you and your computer still be speaking?

Like our experience with the negative "feedback loops" in the environment, we are now running into negative "feedback loops" involving people's reactions to what is done to them by "the system."

Question: Will the little guy continue to pay his taxes when he learns the big guys don't?

Question: Can a political system be drained of credibility the way wells can go dry when a water table recedes?

Question: What happens to the liquidity of the stock market when small investors drop out because they have come to suspect that "insider information" never includes them?

Finally our field of vision for decision-making must come to include the emotional and the aesthetic. To a rational, scientific culture these seem vague and elusive as the morning mist. They are not quantifiable but like the mist they are pervasive. Loyalty, trust, legitimacy, authority are all rooted in emotion and all "matter" when a decision is being made. So does the aesthetic sense of life's beauty or quality or rightness or fitness.

Emotions and aesthetics are real because, despite our efforts to deny or suppress or ignore them, they are still a part of the whole of every human being. They are not only real, they are powerful. And when they are suppressed, they bubble up again in a counter-culture, in gurus, in encounter groups, in "speaking with tongues" or in witchcraft, in demonstrations, and in a host of other similar contemporary phenomena.

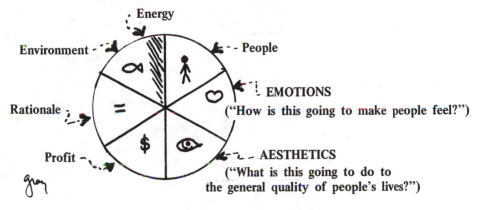

What we have "left out" Theodore Roszak describes very compellingly in his book Where the Wasteland Ends. He speaks of our

> . . . awakening from "single vision and Newton's sleep,"
> where we have dreamt that only matter and history are real.
> This has been the bad, mad ontology of our culture,
> and from it derives that myth of objective consciousness
> which has densified the transcendent symbols and persuaded
> us to believe in the reality of nothing that cannot be weighed
> and measured -- not even our own soul, which is after all a
> subtle dancer. So long as that myth rules the mind, not even
> the most humanely intentioned among us will find any course to
> follow but roads that lead deeper into the wasteland. *

Jonas Salk also speaks of our learning again to take equally seriously all of the aspects of human selfhood:

> A large part of the difficulty of the human condition is due
> to the dissociation between intellect and intuition, a division
> that has been greatly exaggerated as knowledge has increased
> and earlier beliefs have been brought into question. (p. 86f.)

> . . . (Man) will have to learn how to join feeling and reason,
> nonverbal and verbal, as well as subjective and objective sources
> of information and problem-solving. (p. 110)

* Theodore Roszak, *Where the Wasteland Ends,* (Garden City, N.Y.: Doubleday & Co., Inc., 1973), p. 421f.

<u>Question:</u> Can we widen the field of vision for our thinking and our decision-making to include the wholeness of the human situation?

<u>Question:</u> Will we survive if we do not?

8.
<u>Can We Think "Whole" Or Only In Parts?</u>

As our field of vision widens to include more, the question emerges of whether we are capable of thinking "whole" enough." As Amory Lovins has written, "The kernel of the incredible tangle of human problems is the Principle of Interrelatedness expressed in such phrases as 'Everything is connected,' 'You can never do just one thing,' and 'only one earth.' "

Barbara Ward and Rene Dubos have also expressed this vision of unity:

. . . It is only in our own day that astronomers, physicists, geologists, chemists, biologists, anthropologists, ethnologists, and archeologists have all combined in a single witness of advanced science to tell us that, in every alphabet of our being, we do indeed belong to a single system, powered by a single energy, manifesting a fundamental unity under all its variations, depending for its survival on the balance and health of the total system.

If this vision of unity -- which is not a vision only but a hard and inescapable scientific fact -- can become part of the common insight of all the inhabitants of planet Earth, then we may find that, beyond all of our inevitable pluralisms, we can achieve just enough unity of purpose to build a human world. *

* Ward, Barbara and Rene Dubos, "Energy and Matter," "The Alphabet of Time," "A Delicate Balance," and "Strategies for Survival" in *Only One Earth: The Care and Maintenance of a Small Planet.* New York: W.W. Norton & Co., 1972.

The implications of such a shift to "seeing whole" is as
basic and far-reaching as the shift from the Ptolemaic to the
Copernican view of the heavens. All our training has taught us to
look at problems in one way -- in terms of their parts.

> --An essential of the scientific method is "reductionism" or
> reducing a problem to component parts, for better examination
> and solution.

> --Our economic system rewards "sub-optimizing" or developing
> something with the single goal of net profit in view with little or
> no concern for side effects in any other part of the human or
> natural scene.

> --Engineering and technology define tasks by focusing narrowly
> upon the problem to be solved, and seldom ask about problems
> which may be created by the solution of some earlier problem.

Thomas Kuhn, writing about The Structure of Scientific Revolutions,
observes that the Ptolemaic paradigm got in the way of our seeing
the reality that the earth always had gone its course around the sun.
"What a man sees depends both upon what he looks at and also what
his previous visual-conceptual experience has taught him to see." (p. 113)

So let us be clear: when we talk of thinking "whole," we are
intending to do something that isn't going to be easy for us or for our
culture to do.

Question: If specialists by definition don't think whole, where and how
do we develop competence in dealing with the whole?

Question: What paradigms for thinking about the life system as a whole
are emerging?   What procedures can help us function systemically
and holistically?

9.
Adjusting to Limits

Limits are perceived in our culture as negative, as a challenge
to our inventive technology and human will, as something to be
broken or overcome or surpassed.   David Dodson Gray has discussed
what limits have meant to us (see "The Human Dimensions of Limiting
Growth" in "Readings).   Testing limits and breaking limits has
helped our culture to achieve many goals.

There is, however, a small category of "immovable" limits. These we live within and accept and seldom, if ever, question or seek to undo. These limits we look upon usually as beneficial in that they provide us with order and are parameters of our human finitude within the natural order. The number of hours in each day is an immovable limit. So is the indefinite but still limited length of a lifetime. The mystery of another's selfhood is a limit. The limits of growth, Gray suggests in "The Human Dimensions of Limiting Growth" (p. 14-18 in "Readings"), will be added to this small category of "immovable limits."

Another suggestive approach to limits upon growth is to be found in a Boston Globe editorial "20 feet tall" (see "Readings."). It portrays a nightmare in which a baby boy keeps on growing in height until he is "20 feet tall." The editorial points out that the boy's life would become impossible, as would everything in the natural world, if its natural mechanisms did not work to stop growth. Cancer is cell growth gone wild.

Jean-Claude Suares

This thinking is suggestive in that it refers us to organic rather than mechanistic paradigms to organize our thought around. If human-kind is a part of the natural cosmos, if this "wholeness" is the structure of human existence, then we have perhaps betrayed ourselves in pondering too long and hard what Lewis Mumford has called "the myth of the machine."

Question: What have been (and what can be) the positive uses of
limits? The negative uses of limits? What has been the
effect of limits upon different epochs? Different groups?
Do we understand these different effects of limits?

Question: Should everyone live under the same limits? Or is there
value to diversity in limits, or even to having indeterminite
(not clearly determined or perceived) limits?

Question: Do we always have to know what a limit is, or is it sometimes enough just to know that there is a limit and it is near?

10.
Redoing Our Sense of Our Relationship with Nature

Modern man's perceived vocation of "mastering nature" seems
to be coming to an end. That life style is bringing humankind to
the brink of ecological disaster. Many voices are calling upon us
to turn into a new way, to discover within a harmonious relationship
with nature a new sense of selfhood and purpose. Jonas Salk in
The Survival of the Wisest (and notice that he does not speak of the
"survival of the strongest or fittest") commends to man the wisdom
of rightly knowing his destiny within nature:

> . . . An attitude will be needed, not of man "against" Nature,
> but of Man "inclusive with" Nature. (p. 4)

> This suggests that in the future it will be necessary for Man
> to relate to Nature complementarily (and) rather than
> exclusively (either/or). For example, when Man began to
> see himself as separate from Nature and tried to conquer,
> subdue, or outdo it by the use of his intellectual powers, and
> by the knowledge and skills he developed, he brought about
> an imbalance between his Being and his Ego. A change occurred
> from a life in which he lived close to, and part of, Nature, to
> one in which he became increasingly separated from it and
> artificially related to it, through his dependence upon the
> many support systems developed for living this way. (p. 79)

Theodore Roszak in Where the Wasteland Ends put it this way:

> We forget that nature is, quite simply, the universal continuum,
> ourselves inextricably included; it is that which mothered us
> into existence, which will outsurvive us, and from which we
> have learned (if we still remember the lesson) our destiny. (p. 7)

AUDUBON

Reprinted by permission of Edwin Lepper

"I like Disneyland better."

The embrace of nature may often have been rough, even murderous, as when nature assumed the formidable aspect of Mother Kali; but it was nonetheless an embrace. Locked within it, mankind found a sense of the human limits which precluded both arrogance and that dispiriting conviction of cosmic absurdity which haunts contemporary culture. (p. 8)

Question: How far back in our thought world does our separation from nature go? How did it come about?

Question: Will recovering meaning in our time involve a return to a sense of relationship with nature, as Roszak suggests?

Daniel Bell sees the need to relate to nature as behind us:

For most of human history, reality was nature, and in poetry and imagination men sought to relate the self to the natural world. Then reality became technics, tools and things made

by men yet given an independent existence outside himself,
the reified world.   Now reality is primarily the social world --
neither nature nor things, only men -- experienced through
the reciprocal consciousness of self and other.   Society itself
becomes a web of consciousness, a form of imagination to
be realized as a social construction.   Inevitably, a post-
industrial society gives rise to a new Utopianism, both engineering
and psychedelic.   Men can be remade or released, both behavior
conditioned or their consciousness altered.   The constraints
of the past vanish with the end of nature and things. (p. 488)

Question: Do you find valid Bell's description of the three stages
of reality? Are the "constraints of the past" really vanishing?

Question: What part does nature have in "thinking whole"?

THE FACE OF REALITY IS BOTH HUMAN AND NATURAL

SELECTED READINGS

Bell, Daniel, "Culture and Consciousness" in The Coming of Post-Industrial Society: A Venture in Social Forecasting. New York: Basic Books, 1973.

Changing Images of Man, Chapter III, "Economic Man: Servant to Industrial Metaphors," and Chapter V, "Characteristics of an Adequate Image of Humankind." Menlo Park, Calif.: Stanford Research Institute, 1973.

Galbraith, John Kenneth, "The Emancipation of Belief," in Economics and the Public Purpose. Boston, Mass.: Houghton Mifflin Co., 1973.

Gray, David Dodson, "The Human Dimensions of Limiting Growth" in Growth and Its Implications for the Future, Vol. 3. Washington: Government Printing Office, 1974.

Gray, Elizabeth Dodson, "Masculine Consciousness and the Problem of Limiting Growth" in Growth and Its Implications for the Future, Vol. 3.

-----, "Psycho-Sexual Roots of Our Ecological Crisis." Unpublished paper, 1975.

Gray, Elizabeth and David Dodson, "Harnessing Our Will to Survive" in Growth and Its Implications for the Future, Vol. 3.

-----, "After the Candyman: Recovering from Energy Addiction" in Growth and Its Implications for the Future, Vol. 3.

Kuhn, Thomas S., "Revolutions as Changes of World View" in The Structure of Scientific Revolutions, 2nd ed. Chicago: University of Chicago Press, 1970.

Strongman, John, "Societal Values and Material Principles Underlying an Equilibrium Society" in Growth and Its Implications for the Future, Vol. 3.

Ward, Barbara and Rene Dubos, "Energy and Matter," "The Alphabet of Time," "A Delicate Balance," and "Strategies for Survival" in Only One Earth: The Care and Maintenance of a Small Planet. New York: W. W. Norton & Co., Inc., 1972.

"20 feet tall." Boston Globe, Mar. 27, 1974.

"Energy: the Crisis That Could Help Us." Christian Science Monitor, Dec. 17, 1973.

9

THE SEARCH FOR ADJUSTMENT MECHANISMS

SUMMARY

1. The Scope of the Problem

2. Toward a Holistic View of Our Adjustment Mechanisms

    2.1 Kinds of Adjustment-Mechanism Components
    2.2 Location of Components
    2.3 Modeling the Relationships among Components

3. The Time That Systems Require to Adjust to Change

    3.1 Outer and Inner Limits
    3.2 What-We-Can-Affect Is Not What-Is-Most-Imminent
    3.3 A Problem with the Time Frames We Usually Use

4. Significant Problems That Need Adjustment Mechanisms

    4.1 Slowing the Rate of Entropy Increase
    4.2 Anticipating and Assessing Risks
    4.3 "Commons" Behavior

1.
The Scope of the Problem

We described earlier two powerful and complex forces for change in our global life system -- technology and the market-and-price mechanism. Both technology and the marketplace are catalysts for adjustment and change that extend to many levels of effect within the whole system.

But neither technology nor the marketplace makes any pretense of viewing the whole of our global life-system. Each does a particular sort of thing, and that thing happens to move a great deal else. Our global life-system is very sensitive and responsive to those particular sorts of effects.

So what humankind is doing affects the global life-system, yet neither of its two major catalysts-for-change views the life-system holistically -- as a system -- and neither one attempts to adjust it or even to understand it as a whole.

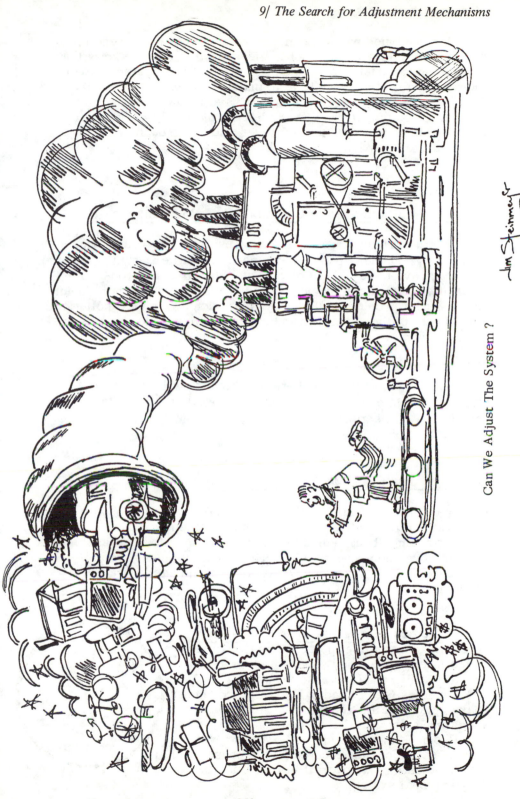

Can We Adjust The System ?

Our continued happy development and evolution depend upon
our relationship with this global life-system. Now we know that
humankind can push and poke on a scale that has system-wide or
global effects. Hence we have to understand what it is we are
doing to the global system. And we have to try to adjust our
actions to be compatible with the health and vitality of this global
life-system upon which our own lives and the growth of our
social-system depend.

2.
Toward a Holistic View of Our Adjustment Mechanisms

We are talking about more than new laws or about having a
few or a great many people do some things differently than before.
We may have to pass laws or change behavior as a stop-gap
measure to put out ecological brushfires. But there is no point
in viewing a problem holistically if you don't also view holistically
the effects of the adjustment mechanisms you might use to solve
that problem.

Question: Where is the holistic thinking we will need before
we even begin to know what might work well at facilitating
the health of the global life system as a whole?

2.1
Kinds of Adjustment-Mechanism Components

In our own attempts to think holistically we have found it
helpful to think of adjustment mechanisms themselves as systems.
In our thinking about them as systems, we have found it useful to
identify three components or functions of adjustment systems and
to reduce these for convenience to simple and easily grasped
symbols.

＊ Meters help us see what is happening.
The U.S. census is a meter. The Consumer
Price Index, the money supply, the Dow-Jones
and the GNP are all meters. The SCEP and
SMIC studies (see "Readings" on Environment)
make quite specific recommendations for
monitoring our global environment.
We also need meters to know how effective
or ineffective our different adjustment mechanisms
are in adjusting our overall impact upon the
larger global system.

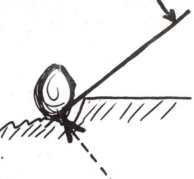

✱ Levers do something that has
a multiplier effect. Like placing a long
prybar under a large boulder, you use
a lever to get leverage. To use a lever
effectively, you have to locate the points
at which the system is going to be
sensitive to pressure from the lever.
Zoning regulations, effluent standards,
subsidies or taxes all are levers.
We use meters to evaluate what levers do.

Question: Are the levers we have effective?
    Do they have the leverage they need
    to be effective?

Question: Are the meters we have effective in monitoring our levers?
    Do the meters simply tell us how the levers are doing? Or
    do they have power to move the levers? (Are the feedback loops
    for controlling action potential but incomplete, or are they
    actually in effect?)

✱ Valves regulate a flow.
A flow is the rate at which a
level or stock of something
accumulates or is disposed of.
The lever as a concept is
concerned with getting something done and with getting
leverage in doing it, but
we tend to think of
levers as getting some-
thing done once and for all.
Valves introduce a
sense of a process of
doing something that continues
over a duration of time.

    An effluent tax is a valve. So is an income tax. So is a
depletion quota. Levers that keep on doing something with a leverage
effect we can also think of as effective valves.

Question: Which sorts of valves are most effective, or are all
    valves functionally alike?

Question: At what points can valves be located? What is the
    effect of the location of a valve upon that valve's effectiveness?
    Are some locations for valves more important than others?
    Are some locations easier to get at than others?

Question: What is the effect of policies that change which meter it is that controls which valve? Are any of these policies stabilizing to the system? Are any destabilizing?

2.2
Location of Components

We have to think about location as well as kinds of functions in an adjustment mechanism for a system. The diagram of the flow of materials shows in schematic form the major stages in the system of flow of useful inputs from the environment through our economic and social system until they are returned to the environment as residuals or waste output from the human system. (For a more detailed treatment of this in a somewhat different form see chapter 1 of Economics and the Environment: A Materials Balance Approach, by Allen V. Kneese, et al., in "Readings.")

Valves and meters can be located to control input policies or output policies at any of the stages in the system.

$$* \; * \; *$$

Input policies at the mine or wellhead could include:

--land-use regulations (Where can this be done?)
--charters (Who is licensed to do this?)
--incentives for new supply (Tax abatements, subsidies, price floors)

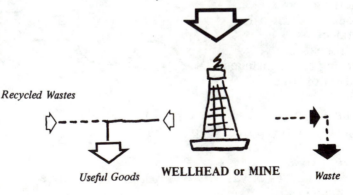

USEFUL INPUT
from the environment

Recycled Wastes

Useful Goods   **WELLHEAD or MINE**   *Waste*

Output policies could affect useful goods output and also waste output.

--depletion quotas (You can only do it so fast.)
--minerals taxes (You have to pay so much of the profit to us.)

At the manufacturing process input policies could include:

--land-use regulations
--materials tax, energy tax (It is more expensive. so use it
    efficiently.)
--charter (Who can be licensed to do this to these inputs?)
--rationing of materials (You can make as much as you can of
    this limited input), rationing of energy.
--incentives for conservation of materials and energy
--restrict loans from banking sources until environmental
    impact statements are filed as supporting documents with loan
    application.

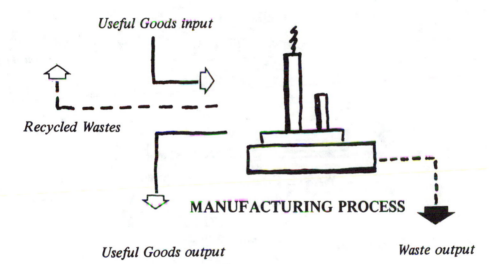

Useful Goods input

Recycled Wastes

MANUFACTURING PROCESS

Useful Goods output

Waste output

Output policies at the manufacturing process level could include:

--tax on final product (It will cost your customers more, so they'll
    use less of it, and you won't profit as much on what you do make.)
--regulation (You can only make this number of them.)
    (They must meet these safety or durability or environmental-
    impact standards.) (You may not discharge this poison at all.)
--effluent tax (You will find it less expensive to pollute less.)
--incentives for recycling, pollution abatement, and non-polluting
    design of manufactured product.

At the consumer level input policies could include:

> --tax on products (They will cost you more, so use less.)
> --rationing (Fewer available and we'll allocate them fairly.)
> --NRU (natural resource unit) pricing
> --incentives for energy conservation (low-cost loans for
>   improving energy efficiency or home insulation)

Useful Goods input

Recycled Wastes

Waste output

CONSUMERS

WASTE COLLECTION POINTS

WASTE OUTPUT
to the environment

gray

Output policies at the consumer level could include:

> --incentives for recycling (We'll pay you for your recyclables.)
> --disincentives for waste (You must pay for what you dispose of.)

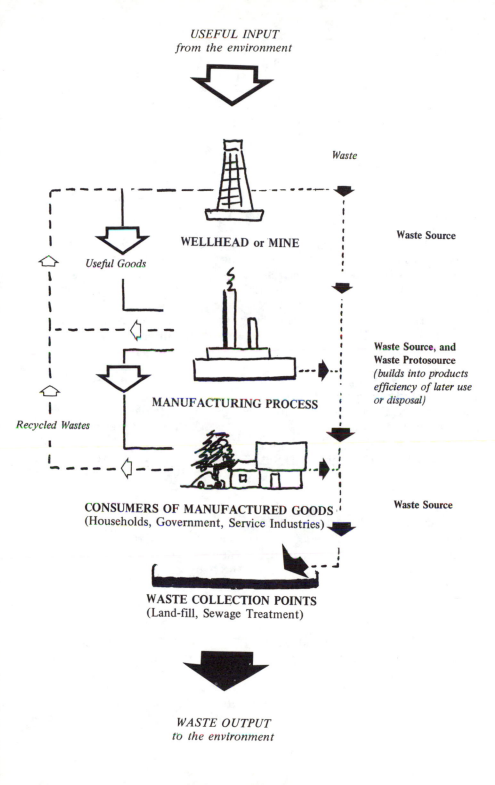

USEFUL INPUT
from the environment

Waste

WELLHEAD or MINE

Waste Source

Useful Goods

MANUFACTURING PROCESS

Waste Source, and
Waste Protosource
(builds into products
efficiency of later use
or disposal)

Recycled Wastes

CONSUMERS OF MANUFACTURED GOODS
(Households, Government, Service Industries)

Waste Source

WASTE COLLECTION POINTS
(Land-fill, Sewage Treatment)

WASTE OUTPUT
to the environment

2.3
Modeling the Relationships among Components

What we have been describing is a very simplified model
of the flow of materials between the environment and the social
system.   It is a characteristic of systems that the whole amounts
to more than the sum of its parts, because together the whole can
do things that the parts by themselves cannot.

Different kinds of modeling get at different features of systems
and are useful for different purposes.

--Allen Kneese and his associates at Resources for the Future,
Inc. use a Materials Balance Approach.

The inputs of the system are fuels, foods, and raw materials
which are partly converted into final goods and partly become
residuals. Except for increases in inventory, final goods
also ultimately enter the residuals stream. Thus, goods which
are "consumed" really only render certain services. Their
material substance remains in existence and must be either
reused or discharged to the natural environment. (p. 7f.
See "Readings.")

--Dale Jorgenson and his associates at Data Resources, Inc.,
have explored the relationship between energy and economic
growth for the Ford Foundation's Energy Policy Project. Their
modeling of these relationships within the U.S. economic and
social system indicate that, by implementing known technology and
placing greater emphasis upon energy conservation, it will be
possible to increase our economic growth faster than our energy-use
rate.

--Edward Goldsmith and his associates who developed the
"Blueprint for Survival" (see 1973 Hearings, p. 331ff.) sought to
formulate "a new philosophy of life, whose goals can be achieved
without destroying the environment, and a precise and comprehensive
programme for bringing about the sort of society in which it can
be implemented." (p. 331.)

--Jay W. Forrester and his M.I.T. associates make models
that seek to reproduce the interactions of different system components
as they change and, in changing, change one another.   This study
of "dynamic interaction" grew out of air-to-air gun control concerns
that after the Korean War were adapted and developed in exploring
the interactions within manufacturing companies of the sales/inventory/

work-force system. It was later extended to urban problems in association with former Mayor John Collins of Boston, and a world model provided the basis for the Limits to Growth report. This sort of modeling does not try to predict the condition of a system at a future date; it explores instead the way the system, as a system, responds to changes which, in changing, are catalysts for many other changes.

Question: What are the advantages and disadvantages of these various modeling efforts?

Question: What are the limits of effectiveness for each effort?

Question: How would each of these modeling efforts be of use in understanding a system we have to live within? In locating and testing adjustment-mechanism components? In planning stages by which to implement an adjustment process whose extent will be unknown until a policy goal or target-level is achieved?

3.
The Time That Systems Require to Adjust to Change

Systems take time to adjust to change. Theory about the market-and-price mechanism assumes it instantaneously adjusts imbalances in supply and demand by price changes. In actual practice the marketplace is seriously limited by time lags. The result is that the market does not adjust large imbalances well at all.

The presence of time lags in any system may tend to destabilize the system by causing the adjustment mechanisms to overcompensate. (Then the system oscillates between feast and famine, over-capacity and under-capacity.) Or the presence of time lags in a system may tend to stabilize the system by damping the responsiveness of the system to transitory changes.

Systems differ, and an important characteristic of systems is the time lags characteristic of the systems. (Systems often have several major and different time lags that separately and together act to affect the system.) The time lags have a great deal to do with how stable or unstable the system is.   And their effect upon system stability itself changes as the system changes, so that time lags that stabilized a system under earlier circumstances may under certain other conditions become destabilizing.

Question: What are some time lags that stabilize our political system in Congress?   That stabilize our social system? Our natural system? What are some time lags that destabilize these systems? Historical examples?

Question: Are we familiar with political time lags that normally stabilize but shift to destabilize a system as that system approaches a limiting condition (an election day, or an impeachment, or both acting upon one another)? Natural time lags that shift from stabilizing to destabilizing? Social time lags that shift like this? Examples?

3.1
Outer and Inner Limits

Amory Lovins in his paper on "Long-Term Constraints on Human Activity" distinguishes between outer limits and inner limits.

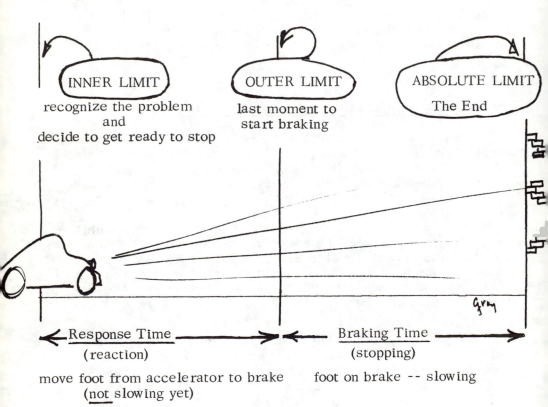

INNER LIMIT
recognize the problem
and
decide to get ready to stop

OUTER LIMIT
last moment to
start braking

ABSOLUTE LIMIT
The End

Response Time
(reaction)

Braking Time
(stopping)

move foot from accelerator to brake   foot on brake -- slowing
(not slowing yet)

(Times and Distances are not to scale)

Because time lags between cause and observed effect are often very long in natural systems, outer limits are important. Once outer limits are passed, the system has a time bomb going.

Question: Have we identified all the potential "time bombs" in our natural system? What long-delayed effects have we identified? Who keeps watch over them? Whose responsibility is it to give early warning? (See "Readings" for proposed National Environmental Policy Institute.)

3.2
What-We-Can-Affect Is Not What-Is-Most-Imminent

Lovins notes that in social and also natural systems, because of the lengths of time it takes for change to take effect in a system, there is usually little except for bandaids that can be done during a crisis to avoid the crisis. What the Titanic needed was not a better lifeboat system, though of course it also needed that. Lovins' point is that the crises we can do something about are ten, fifteen, and more years hence.

Question: Can we identify crises that are not crises yet and won't be for a decade or more? If we identify them, are we very good at knowing how to take action to avoid them? Are there historical examples of prudent foresight and preventive action?

Lovins notes that this reverses the usual procedure of the pragmatic problem-solver. What is most urgent is not what is imminent, because you can do so little about today's crises.

3.3
A Problem with the Time Frames We Usually Use

The man-in-the-street assumes that "someone" is thinking about our system's future in the same way he is thinking about his own and his family's future. He does not realize that for business planning "intermediate-term" means the next year to 18 months, while long-term means usually five or at most eight years ahead. The time frame is largely determined by the length of time presidents of companies are in that office. This usually is no longer than five to eight years, and as a man nears the end of his term, the time frame for responsibility similarly shortens.

Similarly the time frame for government is conditioned by tenure in office or the time until the next election. The longer term is viewed only as a series of these shorter terms, and it is difficult to think constructively about the long term, when one must be preoccupied by successive efforts to win short term elections.

It is instructive here to ponder Man's impact in time and how that impact has been extended by technology:

MAN'S IMPACT IN TIME

I. Impact of One Generation in Pioneer Times

example: a woodlot

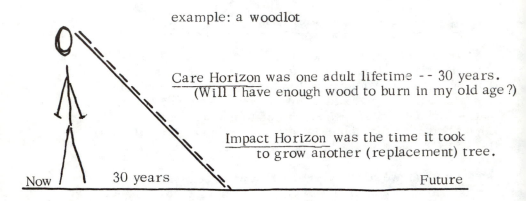

Care Horizon was one adult lifetime -- 30 years.
(Will I have enough wood to burn in my old age?)

Impact Horizon was the time it took
to grow another (replacement) tree.

Now   30 years   Future

In Pioneer Times "Care Horizon" equalled "Impact Horizon"

Man's technology did not enable him to have much impact beyond his own lifetime or "care time"

II. The Impact of One Generation Today -- Because of Technology

example: nuclear energy and its radioactive Plutonium byproduct
(half-life in excess of 24,000 years)

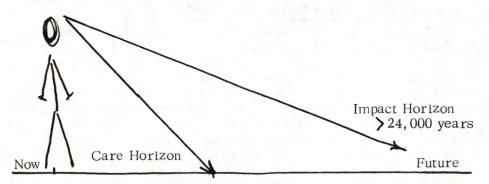

Impact Horizon
> 24,000 years

Now   Care Horizon   Future

With Our Technology Man Today Can Cast a Long Impact Shadow
Past Our Own Lifetime or Care Time

III. The Problem: "Don't Care Time"

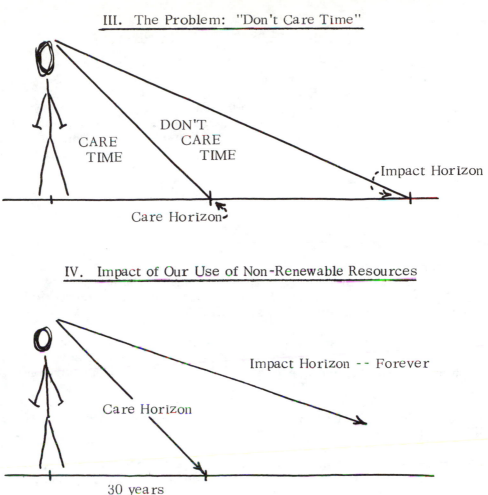

CARE TIME

DON'T CARE TIME

Impact Horizon

Care Horizon

IV. Impact of Our Use of Non-Renewable Resources

Impact Horizon -- Forever

Care Horizon

30 years

Using Up Our Non-Renewable Resources Is a Forever Choice.

(The concepts and original sketch was done by Newell Mack of the M.I.T. seminar. This elaboration of them was done by Elizabeth Dodson Gray. See in the "Readings" Newell Mack's essay "Do Grandchildren Have Rights?" and his proposal for Grandchild Impact Statements, a Grandchild Protection Agency, and a Grandchild Rights Amendment to the Constitution.)

Question: What can we do about "don't-care time"?

Question: How do we balance the interests of today's generation against the interests of future generations when our interests and theirs are not the same? For example, fossil fuels we consume today they won't consume tomorrow because using up non-renewables is "a forever" choice.

4.
Significant Problems That Need Adjustment Mechanisms

We have been talking about adjustment mechanisms and
their components, and also about the systems of which they are
functioning parts. There are in our social and natural systems
some persistent and significant problems which seem to have no
adjustment mechanisms. What controls exist are diffuse, without
great leverage, or they work at times and points in the system to
which the system seems currently unresponsive. These are our
emerging new crises.

4.1
Slowing the Rate of Entropy Increase

Shortages of energy and raw materials are not simply matters
of adequate supply to balance current demand. In the not so long
run this is a matter of the availability of substances in concentrated
enough form to be profitable to use.

Neither the market-and-price mechanism nor profit-oriented
technology is capable of anticipating and responding to this sort of
problem in a time frame whose "don't-care time" to impact horizon
is so large.

Question: Whose business is the question of the rate at which we
use (and use up) raw materials and energy?

Question: Whose business is the question of the inheritance we leave
those who come after us? Whose business is our stewardship of
our birthright?

Question: Has each generation the right to do as it will with the globe,
leaving those who come after to do what they can with what they're
given? Is this a right we have but don't have to use -- like suicide?
Or is this a right that is in any way enforceable? Should it be
enforceable? How? Whose responsibility could this be?

4.2
Anticipating and Assessing Risks

There needs to be a reserve of time in which to adjust to limiting
situations. We are not now accustomed to planning for reserves of
time in the way in which we plan wildlife reserves or reserves of
essential materials.

Question: How do we "stockpile" time the way we stockpile reserves of other essentials for meeting crises?

Question: Whose business is it now to identify irreversible damage, and to see that early warning is given and then initiate corrective action? Who decides now if the irreversible damage "matters"?

As our space and time become more congested, "breathing room" becomes more and more scarce and also precious. We will not be able to regard "time to cope" as a "free good" but as a "depletable resource" that must be valued and conserved.

"My boy, someday none of this will be yours!"

Editorial cartoon by John Fischetti.
Courtesy of Field Newspaper Syndicate.

4.3
"Commons" Behavior

Our natural and social systems are vulnerable to exploitation by individuals in ways that maximize the good of the individual at the expense of the good of the whole. This was labeled "commons behavior" by Garrett Hardin in his essay "The Tragedy of the Commons" (Science, Dec. 13, 1968).

The Rockefeller Land-Use study was the first to recognize land-use as a commons problem and to propose a series of mechanisms to adjust the problem with regard to land use. They propose (1) required impact statements for all changes in land use ("development"); and (2) a change in legal doctrine away from the presumption that the individual owner's rights to development are paramount and that development will be good for the whole, and toward the presumption that the community and environment have rights that are paramount in the face of development.

Question: What other legal doctrines and states of consciousness need to be changed in order to balance better the rights of the individual and the survival needs of the whole?

Cartoon by Jules Feiffer. Reprinted by permission of Field Newspaper Syndicate.

SELECTED READINGS

Models

Beek, W. J., et al., Work for the Future. The Hague, Netherlands: Stichting Maatschappij en Onderneming, 1973.

Kneese, Allen V., et al., "Perspective" in Economics and the Environment: A Materials Balance Approach. Baltimore: Johns Hopkins Press, 1970.

Proposed Adjustment Mechanisms

Congress, A Bill "To amend the National Environmental Policy Act of 1969 to fund and establish a nonprofit National Environmental Policy Institute, and for other purposes." Discussion Draft. 93d Congress, 1st Session.

Lodge, George Cabot, "Change in the Corporations." Harvard Today, Winter 1973.

Mack, Newell B., "Do Grandchildren Have Rights?" in Growth and Its Implications for the Future, Vol. 3. Washington: Government Printing Office, 1974.

-----, "Grandchild-Rights Amendment" in Growth and Its Implications for the Future, Vol. 3.

Musial, John J. and Joseph L. Stearns, "Gasoline Rationing as a Solution to Resource, Environmental and Urban Problems." Journal of Environmental Studies, 1973. Vol. 5, pp. 173-181.

Oregon, State of: Office of the Governor, "Cosmic Economics." March 1974. Prepared by the Center for Applied Energetics.

-----, Energy and State Government: A Decision-Making System Designed to Integrate Social, Economic, and Environmental Processes. July 1, 1973.

Westman, Walter E. and Roger M. Gifford, "Environmental Impact: Controlling the Overall Level." Science, August 31, 1973.

Woodrow Wilson International Center for Scholars, "A Proposal for Developing a Capability at the National Level for Strategic Policy Assessments." August 9, 1973.

Choices

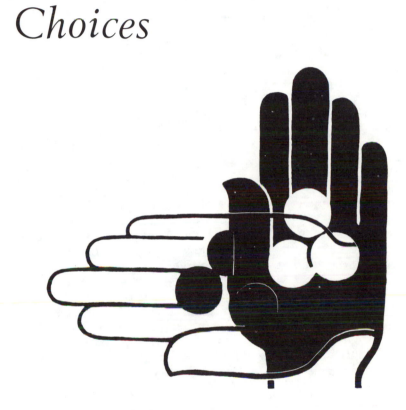

It's in your hands.

1.
A Time for Choices

Jonas Salk writes of Man as standing at a fork-in-the-road in the cultural evolutionary processes. Nelson Rockefeller, after leaving the governorship of New York, initiated and chaired a project on "Critical Choices for Americans." The Ford Foundation Energy Policy Project on alternative energy options presents its findings in three scenarios or futures. The Stanford Research Institute report on Changing Images of Man foresees two major alternative future images of humankind.*

One choice always involves continuing as we have been -- "historical growth" as the Energy Policy Project labels it. Changing Images of Man calls it our "technological extrapolationist future." The alternatives to "business as usual" involve one or another significant change in either or both our ways of thinking and our ways of living.

2.
The Present Direction

The tremendous weight of inertia present in the movement of human systems makes it very easy and natural to continue on as we are. The problem with business-as-usual is that it may lead us to some places and ways of life we would not choose if we were given a conscious choice. For example:

If the post-industrial era of the future is dominated by the industrial-era premises, images, and policies of the past, the control of deviant behavior needed to make societal regulation possible would in all likelihood require the application of powerful socio- and psycho-technologies.

The result could well be akin to what has been termed "friendly fascism" -- a managed society which rules by a faceless and widely dispersed complex of warfare-welfare-industrial-communications-police bureaucracies with a technocratic ideology. (Images, p. vi. Italics added.)

---

* Jonas Salk, *The Survival of the Wisest* (1973), p. 5. *Exploring Energy Choices,* A Preliminary Report of the Ford Foundation Energy Policy Project (April 1974). *Changing Images of Man,* A Stanford Research Institute Policy Research Report (October 1973).

Robert Heilbroner, in his sobering book <u>The Human Prospect</u> (1974), puts it like this:

> . . . (T)he passage through the gauntlet ahead may be possible only under governments capable of rallying obedience far more effectively than would be possible in a democratic setting. (p. 110).

Scott Paradise states it well in his introduction to Prospects for Massachusetts Tomorrow: Toward a Discussion of Alternatives:

> Critical decisions about the kind of long-term future we want for ourselves and our posterity must and will be made in the next few years. . . . <u>To do nothing is a choice to let the system take its own course.</u> <u>We cannot avoid choices about the future of our state.</u> (p. 1. Italics added.)

3.
Alternatives

The various papers in the "Readings" present a veritable smorgasbord of recent thinking about choices.

Social Planning: Daniel Bell has a chapter from his book <u>The Coming of Post-Industrial Society</u> on "Social Choice and Social Planning: The Adequacy of Our Concepts and Tools." On a state level Scott Paradise, the director of Massachusetts Tomorrow, Inc., presents two alternative futures for Massachusetts. On the national level Joseph Perkowski and Anthony Picardi develop a series of specific "Goals and Policies for a Sustainable Society."

How We Organize Our Lives and Work: Frank Basler focuses upon our bureaucratic way of organizing and sees problems ahead. He explores new alternatives in his "Options for Coping with Organizational Stresses in a Limited-Growth Future." A chapter from <u>Changing Images of Man</u> asks about "Societal Choices and Consequences of Changing Images."

Choices about Sharing: David and Elizabeth Dodson Gray anticipated the April 1974 demands by the Have-Not nations at the Special UN General Assembly that the Have nations "share the wealth." In "Sharing the Pie" Elizabeth Gray explores what possible self-interest there could be for the rich to share the pie more equitably than at present. In "The Misplaced Zero-Sum Game" David and Elizabeth Dodson Gray use game theory to sort out the differing kind of choices we face in the biosphere and ethosphere.

Choices about the Future of Humankind: Robert L. Heilbroner in two sections from <u>The Human Prospect</u> summarizes our predicament and sees a dim future ahead for humankind. Jonas Salk in the last three chapters from his book <u>The Survival of the Wisest</u> discusses wisdom as the "new kind of fitness" for survival. Arnold Toynbee discusses "The Challenge of Tomorrow" and sees extinction as the penalty for unlimited economic growth.

4.
The Survival of the Wisest

The thesis underlying many of these studies is that in order to survive humankind is going to have to revise our present way of life. Jonas Salk has written:

In a sense, Man is like the Frankenstein monster. He has been produced by the process of evolution itself, to which he now contributes actively. Constructed for fitness to survive under previously prevailing circumstances, he must now accommodate to new conditions of life that are radically different quantitatively and qualitatively, for which he is, in part, responsible. Through the evolutionary processes that have produced him, Man and Nature together are now, in effect, the joint authors of the human predicament. (p. 117)

In the epoch before us Salk foresees a survival not of the strongest but of the wisest. For Salk, "Wisdom (is) the art of the disciplined use of imagination in respect to alternatives. . . ." (p. 72) "Wisdom implies making judgments in advance rather than retrospectively, and this is the test which Man now faces." (p. 110)

5.
Wisdom Implies Judgments in Advance

For developing wisdom to survive, it is crucial to ponder thought-fully and imaginatively the choices before us, and try to think ourselves into "alternative futures." The race is not always to the swift or to the biggest, but to the most adaptable. Dinosaurs, despite their great size, did not survive -- did not <u>adapt</u> -- to a change in the climate of their time.

"Look, kid, we're aware of the problems besetting our society. We're working on them."

The question facing us is this:

Can we ponder in a disciplined way our choices of alternative futures so that we <u>can</u> adapt and survive?

For the gravity of the human prospect does not hinge alone, or even principally, on an estimate of the dangers of the knowable external challenges of the future. To a greater extent it is shaped by our appraisal of our capacity to meet those challenges. *

---

* Robert Heilbroner, *An Inquiry into the Human Prospect*, p. 24.

SELECTED READINGS

Social Planning

Bell, Daniel, "Social Choice and Social Planning: The Adequacy of Our Concepts and Tools" in The Coming of Post-Industrial Society: A Venture in Social Forecasting. New York: Basic Books, Inc., 1973.

Paradise, Scott I., "Prospects for Massachusetts Tomorrow: Toward a Discussion of Alternatives." Cambridge, Mass.: Massachusetts Tomorrow, Inc., 1974.

Perkowski, Joseph and Anthony Picardi, "Evaluating Goals for a Sustainable Society" in Growth and Its Implications for the Future, Vol. 3. Washington: Government Printing Office, 1974.

How We Organize Our Lives and Work

Basler, Frank, "Options for Coping with Organizational Stresses in a Limited-Growth Future" in Growth and Its Implications for the Future, Vol. 3.

"Societal Choices and Consequences of Changing Images" in Changing Images of Man. Menlo Park, Calif.: Stanford Research Institute, 1973.

Choices about Sharing

Gray, Elizabeth Dodson, "Sharing the Pie: New Perspectives upon Self-Interest" in Growth and Its Implications for the Future, Vol. 3.

Gray, Elizabeth and David Dodson, "The Misplaced Zero-Sum Game" in Growth and Its Implications for the Future, Vol. 3.

Choices about the Future of Humankind

Heilbroner, Robert L., An Inquiry into the Human Prospect. New York: W. W. Norton & Co., Inc., 1974.

Salk, Jonas, "Cosmic Perspective," "To Behave 'As If'," and "Wisdom -- A New Kind of Fitness" in The Survival of the Wisest. New York: Harper and Row, 1973.

Toynbee, Arnold, "The Challenge of Tomorrow: Extinction Is the Penalty for Unlimited Economic Expansion." Japan Times, October 6, 1972.

MEMORANDUM

JUNE 14, 1974.

To: Members, Committee on Merchant Marine and Fisheries
From: Leonor K. Sullivan, Chairman
Subject: Committee Hearings on Growth and Its Implications for the
Future.

In the course of this Congress, our Committee has initiated an intensive examination of growth-related issues and their implications for the future of this country. Our reason for doing so stems from the very close relationship between these questions and their environmental manifestations.

In these investigations we have been working very closely with academic, business and environmental organizations. The first hearings on the general topic were held last May, and the hearings have recently been reopened on particular growth questions.

One of the principal resources which has been made available to the Committee has been a series of papers prepared by members of a seminar, conducted at the Sloan School of Management, MIT, by Dr. Carroll L. Wilson. Those papers, together with related readings, have recently been published as Parts 2 and 3 of our hearing record. Part 1, which involved last year's hearings together with an extensive appendix, proved to be very popular, and the Committee's stocks were rapidly exhausted. We have every reason to believe that Parts 2 and 3 will be at least as popular.

Because the papers themselves, without the attached readings, sketch a brief but comprehensive outline of these problems and because I believe that the implications of these questions for the future are profound, I have taken the unusual step of arranging for these to be printed as a separate Committee Print. Copies of the complete set, Parts 2 and 3, are available to you upon request.

I believe that this Print, and the issues which it identifies, merit careful examination by every Member of the Committee and the Congress. Certainly there are points at which I, or any of us, might differ with the authors of these papers, dealing as they do with complex issues, value judgments and ambiguous signposts to the future. But the questions involved are important and affect and are affected by decisions that we are making almost daily—or are refusing to make, which amounts to the same thing.

No institution is available to us today to help us judge the long-range implications of decisions now made on a short-term, *ad hoc* basis. That we should improve our ability to foresee these implications can scarcely be questioned, although how this should be done is far from clear. I believe that the lucid and coherent statement of the problem, contained in this Committee Print, may serve a useful purpose by putting these matters into perspective and, at the very least, by giving us a clearer conception of the problems that already confront us, or that may soon do so.

I commend this Print to your attention; I believe that it will more than repay your review.

INTRODUCTION

WASHINGTON, D.C., *May 28, 1974.*

Hon. LEONOR K. SULLIVAN,
Chairman, Committee on Merchant Marine and Fisheries,
House of Representatives, Washington, D.C.

DEAR MADAM CHAIRMAN: With your active support and encouragement, the Subcommittee on Fisheries and Wildlife Conservation and the Environment held hearings on the general topic of growth and its implications for the future of this country. In the course of these hearings, it became clear that this topic is one of profound importance today, to which surprisingly little attention has been given, particularly with respect to potential mechanisms for dealing with the problem.

We had invited Dr. Carroll L. Wilson, a distinguished professor at the Sloan School of Management, MIT, to participate in the 1973 hearings, but his schedule did not allow him to do so. Dr. Wilson did, however, express an active interest in the subject matter of the hearings and met on several occasions with the staff of the Committee to discuss ways in which he might be of further assistance.

Dr. Wilson has a graduate seminar at MIT which has been studying, over the past two years, the implications of a society in the process of reacting a mode of sustainable growth. I asked him if he would make the talents of his students available to the Committee, and he promptly accepted the challenge.

The results of his seminar's activities are most impressive. They have factored into their efforts the product of the first of our hearings, printed last year as Part I, and the issues and questions posed in the course of those hearings. With the insight produced by intensive review of these issues, they have refined the questions and have pointed up the essential nature of the conflicts which must be faced as we begin to develop strategies to deal with these new and difficult problems.

The product of these activities is enclosed. I suggest that it be printed as Parts II and III of our hearings on growth and its implications for the future, and that it be used as the foundation for the next series of hearings on this subject, which we hope to convene later in the year.

You will note that the organization of this work lends itself very well to this format. After a brief introduction to some of the essential concepts involved, each section of the report contains a discussion of the issue involved, followed by a series of readings and relevant newspaper stories on the general topic. An effort was made to see that all sides of a given controversy were presented, since it was clearly not the intention of the seminar to dictate the conclusions which must be reached, any more than it is our intention to accept any such conclusions without debate. Indeed, the principal purpose of our publishing these papers would be to provide a focal point for enlightened debate on these matters in the future.

As presented to the Committee, the documents fall into two categories: the first, entitled "The Parameters of Growth," discusses some of the points at which growth-related problems impact society and constrain decisions which must be made to cope with these problems. The second, entitled "How Well Will our Adjustment Mechanisms Work?" discusses some of the means which society has or must develop to deal with these problems.

The cumulative message presented by these issue papers and readings is by no means new or startling; it has been stated often, but never so well as by Garrett Hardin in his book *Exploring New Ethics for Survival:* "You can never do merely one thing".

I understand that the story of the blind men sent to describe an elephant, in which each concludes that the animal resembles only what he himself has experienced, is not peculair to our own culture and that comparable fables are found in other cultures and times. Perhaps this is fortunate, because it carries a moral with acute relevance; not only may the whole be greater than the sum of its parts, but it may also differ from the sum of its parts. And this I believe to be an important message indeed.

Specialists abound in any high-technology civilization—such civilizations depend upon highly trained individuals who understand a great deal about fairly narrow subjects. The problem then becomes one of being able to comprehend the implications of these specialties and relating these to the goals of the civilization itself; this task has never yet received a high priority. One message from the seminar is clear, and I think that few will dissent; we need to develop people who are trained as generalists—who are able to look at complicated, interrelated problems and develop strategies to resolve these problems which do not defeat the very ends which they seek.

Probably the most significant aspect of the dilemma which confronts us is that no single issue, or even kind of issue, lies at its heart. It is perfectly true that overpopulation is a major element and it is just as true that other elements include the consequences of specialized or partial technologies, and also the human element described in Hardin's seminal essay, "The Tragedy of the Commons": that individuals tend to reach decisions which are optimal for themselves, but are decidedly suboptimal for society. While these statements are true enough, they are only partially effective as answers: there is no easy handle by which we can grasp these elements of the problem and weld them into a tool to resolve that same problem, but this is the job that we face. These conflicts *must* be resolved in order for society to make the transition to a different, hopefully better and more just, society which may be sustained over a long run.

It is this question to which the attached papers are directed: how are we to do this, assuming that we agree that it should be done? To pose the question in this fashion, of course, makes a clearly stated basic assumption: that it is desirable that we should achieve a sustainable, or steady-state, society. I am not altogether certain that everyone shares this view. To put it another way, we have and demonstrate some concern for the welfare and happiness of our children, but tend to discount heavily the elements which bear upon the welfare of *their* children. The real question which we face today is how much are we prepared to sacrifice for those generations yet unborn?

Even if we are disposed to act with the welfare of our grandchildren in view, a derivative question becomes just how are our choices today relevant to those grandchildren? That they are relevant, there can be no doubt, but society does not appear to be equipped to make institutional decisions that carry a sound underpinning of analysis of their long-term implications. The bill which you and I have jointly introduced, H.R. 14468, addresses itself to this issue. I am not satisfied that the bill has all the answers, but it certainly appears to be moving in the right direction.

I believe that the publication of the attached documents will serve to advance, to a considerable extent, the dialogue on these important questions. They point to no easy conclusions because there are no easy conclusions, but they do clarify and explicate the issues and in so doing perform an important service. We will seek, in the hearings which we hope to hold later in the year, to continue this process.

Sincerely,

JOHN D. DINGELL,
Chairman, Subcommittee on Fisheries and
Wildlife Conservation and the Environment.

FOREWORD

Background of the M.I.T. Seminar on Sustainable Growth

It was in March of 1972 that *The Limits to Growth* by Meadows et al presented some implications of continuing exponential growth of population, capital investment, natural resource depletion and pollution. Since then over a million copies in translations into 18 languages have stirred controversy and raised awareness everywhere.

In the summer of 1972 it seemed useful to explore some Strategies for Sustainable Growth, and the method of a continuing seminar at M.I.T. was chosen as a way of trying to identify what kinds of social, political and economic systems might be visualized which might achieve and maintain an equilibrium with the biosphere.

One of the early discoveries was that there was almost no literature. Very few people had turned their attention to these problems. This situation made it attractive and effective to gather together a varied group of individuals—students and others—who brought well-trained, creative and interactive minds to bear on this pioneering task. Assuming that exponential growth must at some point cease or lead to ecological disaster, we decided to investigate environmentally sustainable modes of growth and to conceptualize models for a future steady-state America. We wondered what the system of values, life-style, technology and form of government in this America would be like. What lessons could be learned from study of the history of earlier societies which had remained stable for long periods of time? Would transition to steady-state be easier in Japan, where an ethic of group action and loyalty takes the place of the American spirit of individualism? We always tried to look beyond the short term and to imagine what life would be like in our grandchildren's lifetime. A series of "Grandchild Impact Statements" were prepared. This took us outside the framework of the argumentative short term question, "Is growth good or bad?" and allowed us to stretch our imaginations toward long-term alternative futures.

The participants over the two-year period have included Frank Basler, William Behrens, Daniel Chin, Rebecca Cook, Richard Gillett, Gregor Goethals, Elizabeth and David Dodson Gray, Steven Green, Newell Mack, Donald MacDougal, William Martin, Leopold Michel, Scott Paradise, Joe Perkowski, Anthony Picardi Nancy Lovett, Henry Richardson, Lisa Riordan, Dale Runge, Charles Savage, Wayne Schneckenburger, John Seegar, John Strongman, Joseph Straley, Tomihiro Taniguchi, Kie Wei Tung, David Weir, Jan-Olaf Willums and Wilbert Wils.

Throughout the past two years the Seminar has attracted a variety of interesting people from the Cambridge community. Participants have included students from M.I.T. and Harvard, fellows from the Episcopal Theological Seminary and visiting professors on sabbatical leave from other universities. Discussions have been enriched by sessions with Chester Cooper, Herman Daly, Garrett Hardin, Hazel Henderson, David Hertz, John Holdren, George Cabot Lodge, and others who have shared our enthusiasm in speculating on alternative futures for the United States.

We have been greatly encouraged by our association with Frank Potter, Counsel for the Committee on Merchant Marine and Fisheries of the House of Representatives and by the leadership provided by Congressman John Dingell in holding hearings on Growth and Its Implications for the Future on May 1, 1973. The unique volume assembled by the Congressional Research Service brought together for the first time much of the relevant literature in this field.

It has been a special privilege this year to turn our attention to a formulation of the issues of policy which might provide a framework for additional hearings which might be held on these subjects. Congressman Dingell graciously accepted our offer of help. We have worked closely with Frank Potter and have had aid and guidance from Wallace Bowman, Harvey Sherman and Clay Wellborn of the Library of Congress.

The Issue Papers have been largely written and illustrated by David and Elizabeth Gray and William Martin with criticism and some editing by William Matthews, Leopold Michel, Joseph Straley and Jill Wheaton.

This Seminar has confirmed my personal conviction that creative contributions towards a better understanding of frontier problems can be made by participants in such a seminar. Moreover, if given the opportunity they can relate these things to the choices in the real world as David and Elizabeth Gray and William Martin have done in the remarkable set of papers they have prepared.

The opportunity to work on the hearings has presented a challenge to us to work back from our speculation on life in our grandchildren's time to the reality of hard core problems of today. It has given us a better glimpse into the complexity and interrelatedness of all the parameters of growth which the Issue Papers aim to show.

If our educational experiment is successful, it becomes particularly rewarding in light of the fact that the America of the 21st century will belong to those who are under thirty today. Young thinkers are often able to peer into the future with a sharpness of vision unequalled by their elders. If the ideas presented in this volume encourage some youthful members of our society to become architects and builders of a sustainable America, then our efforts and the efforts of Congress will have been handsomely rewarded. If hope can displace despair, and impulses both strong and creative can be unleashed, life in the 21st century will be a "magnificent experiment."

CARROLL L. WILSON.

The original two-volume report to Congress contains most of the suggested "Readings" and is Serial No. 93-28 and 93-29. Available from the Superintendent of Documents, U. S. Government Printing Office, Washington, D. C. 20402.   Approximately $15.

ORDER FORM

To order an additional copy or copies of:

GROWTH AND ITS IMPLICATIONS FOR THE FUTURE

please write, or tear out this page as your handy order form.

Kindly send me _____ copies of

quantity

GROWTH AND ITS IMPLICATIONS FOR THE FUTURE

Name _____

Address _____

_____

City_____ State _____ Zip _____

I enclose $ _____ with this order. *(No C.O.D.'s please)*

Each copy: $3.95, plus postage & handling $.30, total $4.25
Two copies: $8.25 Three copies: $12.25

　　Conn. residents add $.28 sales tax per copy.

Quantity discounts:

　　10–19 copies, ordered at one time: 15% discount plus a
　　　　free teacher's copy.

　　20 or more copies, ordered together: 25% discount plus
　　　　a free teacher's copy.

Fold here Fold here

Postage

Stamp

TO: **THE DINOSAUR PRESS**
          P. O. Box 666
          Branford, Connecticut 06405

Fold here Fold here

ORDER FORM

To order an additional copy or copies of:

GROWTH AND ITS IMPLICATIONS FOR THE FUTURE

please write, or tear out this page as your handy order form.

Kindly send me _____ copies of
  quantity

GROWTH AND ITS IMPLICATIONS FOR THE FUTURE

Name _____

Address _____

_____

City_____ State_____ Zip_____

I enclose $ _____ with this order. *(No C.O.D.'s please)*

Each copy: $3.95, plus postage & handling $.30, total $4.25
Two copies: $8.25   Three copies: $12.25

  Conn. residents add $.28 sales tax per copy.

Quantity discounts:

  10–19 copies, ordered at one time: 15% discount plus a
      free teacher's copy.

  20 or more copies, ordered together: 25% discount plus
      a free teacher's copy.

Fold here   *Fold here*

Postage

Stamp

TO: **THE DINOSAUR PRESS**
       P. O. Box 666
       Branford, Connecticut 06405

Fold here   *Fold here*

ORDER FORM

To order an additional copy or copies of:

GROWTH AND ITS IMPLICATIONS FOR THE FUTURE

please write, or tear out this page as your handy order form.

Kindly send me _____ copies of
quantity

GROWTH AND ITS IMPLICATIONS FOR THE FUTURE

Name _____

Address _____

_____

City_____ State_____ Zip_____

I enclose $_____ with this order.   *(No C.O.D.'s please)*

Each copy: $3.95, plus postage & handling $.30, total $4.25
Two copies: $8.25   Three copies: $12.25

    Conn. residents add $.28 sales tax per copy.

Quantity discounts:

    10–19 copies, ordered at one time: 15% discount plus a
        free teacher's copy.

    20 or more copies, ordered together: 25% discount plus
        a free teacher's copy.

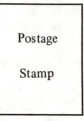

Postage

Stamp

TO: **THE DINOSAUR PRESS**

P. O. Box 666

Branford, Connecticut 06405

ORDER FORM

To order an additional copy or copies of:

GROWTH AND ITS IMPLICATIONS FOR THE FUTURE

please write, or tear out this page as your handy order form.

Kindly send me _____ copies of
                  quantity

GROWTH AND ITS IMPLICATIONS FOR THE   FUTURE

Name _____

Address _____

_____

City_____ State _____ Zip_____

I enclose $ _____ with this order. *(No C.O.D.'s please)*

Each copy: $3.95, plus postage & handling $.30, total $4.25
Two copies: $8.25 Three copies: $12.25

   Conn. residents add $.28 sales tax per copy.

Quantity discounts:

   10–19 copies, ordered at one time: 15% discount plus a
      free teacher's copy.

   20 or more copies, ordered together: 25% discount plus
      a free teacher's copy.

Postage

Stamp

TO: **THE DINOSAUR PRESS**
P. O. Box 666
Branford, Connecticut 06405